Three IN One

UNSOLVED MYSTERIES OF THE BIBLE FROM GENESIS TO REVELATION

Mark Anthony Grubb

ISBN 979-8-88540-542-3 (paperback)
ISBN 979-8-88540-543-0 (digital)

Christian Faith Publishing
832 Park Avenue
Meadville, PA 16335
www.christianfaithpublishing.com

Printed in the United States of America

Contents

PREFACE

When I was about nine years old, I was baptized in a Baptist church. My father had abandoned my mom when I was only two months old and was the baby of six children. My mother was one of the most spiritual women of faith I have ever known. She was my spiritual rock and made sure I was in the church at least every Sunday and Sunday night. From the time I was just a boy, I have had several close and personal encounters with the supernatural. Please save any reservations you have for that word of choice until you have read this book in its entirety. All considerations of accuracy have been reassured by the only source of truth we have ever had, which is the Word of God.

In my young and maturing mind, I had no clue as to why these particular things were happening to me and around me. However, these things did not leave my mind nor my presence into adulthood. Some of these things changed into manifestations that others around me could observe. As I proceeded through my long research of God's Word, digging into his truth like a biblical archeologist, something became profoundly clear. With each shovel of truth, I overturned my lifelong experiences became more and more tangible. These unknown mysteries that captivated me became realistic. Memories became factual instead of some conjured nonsense that resulted from watching movies or reading the wrong literature. As I evoke and recall these experiences, please know that this book is not about fiction. The content of my life experiences did not collide negatively with the Bible. The Bible confirmed them in many ways. Of course, as a child, my heart could not remotely understand what my mind and my reasoning had not been taught. This took time. Time is the misty state of our existence in which we all presently reside.

We are living entities riding upon the rotating atoms and molecules that God our Father and creator of all things made, and it is only our temporary carnal state of being.

There have been many mysteries in the Bible that have spiritually haunted me for most of my life. I have sought the answers through various sources, including theology, literature, and many conversations with men of the cloth. Most conversations of which were in part just a personal opinion or the discipline of a particular doctrine or school of thought or science. Some of the answers offered to me were in disagreement with what I had learned from other sources. Even though I sought the truth and read my Bible, the answers were not remotely clear to me. Several times, Satan had convinced me that there wasn't a real source for the answer to the mysteries I wanted to resolve. He relentlessly insisted that the mysteries I was trying to unravel were never intended to be solved. I became uninterested in any spiritual things by the time I was in my forties. Occasionally, I would go to different churches to see if I could regain that zeal and passion for the Lord and the truth. However, spiritually speaking, I had become a dead man walking. Every time there was even a notion of my faith being resurrected, Satan was jolly on the spot to subdue me. Then suddenly in the autumn of my life, God reminded me of Satan's true nature. "Ye are of your father the devil, and the lusts of your father ye will do. He was a murderer from the beginning, and abode not in the truth, because there is no truth in him. When he speaketh a lie, he speaketh of his own: for he is a liar and the father of it" (John 8:44). Biblical scholars and theologians have offered varying interpretations of the meaning and significance of many scriptures. What you will read within the confines of this book, I trust, are several mysteries or unanswered questions you have had just like myself. Together, we will discover the answers to those unanswered questions. They are of no private interpretation. Language is the substance of God since we read in *John 1:1 (KJV)*, "In the beginning was the Word, and the Word was with God, and the Word was God." We discover that "God is" many things on our truth journey. "He that loveth not knoweth not God; for God is love" (1

John 4:8 KJV). God is the creator and the author of all things. Let us begin our journey.

"We were spirits beckoned by the passion of a moment and we the unborn begin our journey of life in our mother's womb and with one gasp of air we were given a name and the power of free will" (Mark Anthony Grubb).

CHAPTER 1

Three in One

What is the difference between the soul and the spirit? I had asked countless Christians if the soul and the spirit were the same things. Of course, I got different answers, but the majority of people concluded that the soul and spirit are interpreted to mean the same thing and end up being used interchangeably. Or is the truth that they are the same yet they are separated by their attributes?

"Is there a difference between the soul and the spirit, and does it matter if there is?" Regardless of what philosophy, literature, religion, or some scientists say, we have to ask, "What does the Bible say?" The Bible makes many references to both. So what does God's Word say about our soul and our spirit? For that matter, what does it say about flesh, body, and soul? And why can knowing this be a crucial factor in our spiritual progress and relationship with God? First Thessalonians 5:23 says, "And the God of peace Himself sanctify you wholly, and may your *spirit* and *soul* and *body* be preserved complete, without blame, at the coming of our Lord Jesus Christ." This verse tells us that human beings are made up of three parts—the spirit, soul, and body. In the original Greek language, the conjunction "and" in "spirit and soul and body" indicates the three are different from one another. So just as the body is separate and distinct from the soul, the soul is also separate and distinct from the spirit. *Hebrews 4:12* makes an even finer distinction, saying, "For the word of God is living and operative and sharper than any two-edged sword, and piercing even to the dividing of *soul* and *spirit* and of joints and marrow, and able to discern the thoughts and intentions of the heart." From this verse, we can understand that the soul and the spirit are so close to one another that the two require the Word of God to divide them and to separate them from each other.

It is time that we break down the three components we all have and share as best we can and at the same time use the only source of truth that we have which is God's Word.

In *1 Thessalonians 5:23*, again, the Word of God strikes a separation of spirit soul and body. "And the very God of peace sanctify you wholly, and I pray God your whole spirit and soul and body be preserved blameless unto the coming of our Lord Jesus Christ."

Based on these two verses alone, we can conclude that our soul and our spirit are not the same things. It is not only important for us to see that they are distinct components, but also to discern one from the other.

We know from God's Word that God the father is a spirit as we read in John 4:24, "God is a spirit and they that worship him must worship him in spirit and truth."

In Genesis 2:7, we read how man becomes a soul: "And the LORD God formed man of the dust of the ground, and breathed into his nostrils the breath of life, and man became a living soul." It is to be noted in later translations of the Bible (such as the NLT, CSB, and NASB) *soul* is replaced by a "living person," which is my opinion errs on the side of a false statement that changes the narrative of God completely. The word *soul* in Hebrew is *neshama*. Man's body became a soul by God's divine breath.

So we know that we must take a closer look or study to know the truth so the truth can set us free (John 8:32). This is necessary so our conclusion can further be based on the truth of God's words. God is the trinity—the Father, Son, and Holy Ghost. God made us unique of all things, including the angels in heaven. We are three in one just as the trinity; although we are the three are one and assigned to only one. Since we are made in God's image, it can be concluded by his word that this indeed is the case for us as well. Let us go to the Bible to see how each part of mankind is almost the same yet different. We need to study to see if one may be required to lead the other and so on. We will learn the facts of the truth of questions never answered. Questions like, "Does God have a soul?" Do you go to heaven when you die? Do spirits need food? I'm glad you joined me on this journey. Perhaps if we can turn over just a handful of things that were unknown or even mysteries to us before we began, then we have met our goal of discovery. "*Study* to shew *thyself approved* unto God, a workman that needeth not to be ashamed, rightly dividing the word of truth" (2 Tim. 2:15 KJV).

Our Soul

Jesus asked a question one time over two thousand years ago for all times. "For what will it profit a man if he gains the whole world and forfeits his soul." We know that Jesus the man also had a soul. "Then saith he unto them, My soul is exceeding sorrowful, even unto death: tarry ye here, and watch with me" (Matt. 26:38 KJV). Or what shall a man give in return for his own soul? (Matt. 16:26 ESV). We will also see that he refers to the spirit. Again, the question. Are the soul and the spirit the same thing and not different at all? Or is there something else?

The scriptures reveal that our soul is home to our emotions our minds and our human free will. The soul is where our sinful nature also resides. It occupies our physical bodies. It is who we are as human beings.

In Genesis 2:7, we read of the moment man become a living soul: "And the LORD God formed man of the dust of the ground, and breathed into his nostrils the breath of life; and man became a living soul."

"For what will it profit a man if he gains the whole world and forfeits his soul? Or what shall a man give in return for his soul?" (Matt. 16:26 ESV). This is Jesus speaking. Our God is a God of emotions. The scriptures reveal all of them.

Love: "Anyone who does not love does not know God, because God is love" (1 John 3:8). God not only feels love he is love. Love is the reason that he sent his son to die for us. "For God. so loved the world that he gave his only begotten son, that whoever believes in him should not perish but have eternal life" (John 3:16). He loves us with an everlasting love. "The LORD appeared to him from far away. I have loved you with an everlasting love; therefore I have continued my faithfulness to you" (Jer. 31:3).

Hate: "There are six things the LORD hates, seven that are detestable to him: haughty eyes, a lying tongue, hands that shed innocent blood, a heart that devises wicked schemes, feet that are quick to rush into evil, a false witness who pours out lies and a person who stirs up conflict in the community" (Prov. 6:16–19 NIV) is not be confused with the seven deadliest sins. We will look at that a little later. "The Lord tests the righteous, *but his soul hates* the wicked and the one who loves violence" (Ps. 11:5 ESV). This verse not only confirms that the Lord hates the wicked and those who love violence, but we receive a clear revelation that states "his soul hates," which is the core of all our emotions. God has a soul, which is not his spirit because we know that "God is a Spirit: and they that worship him must worship him in spirit and in truth" (John 4:24).

Jealousy: "You shall not bow down to them or serve them, for I the LORD your God am a jealous God, visiting the iniquity of the fathers on the children to the third and the fourth generation of those who hate me" (Exod. 20:5). But Joshua said to the people, "You are not able to serve the LORD, for he is a holy God. He is a jealous God; he will not forgive your transgressions or your sins" (Josh. 24:19).

Joy: "For as a young man marries a young woman, so shall your sons marry you, and as the bridegroom rejoices over the bride, so shall your God rejoice over you" (Isa. 62:5 ESV). "I will rejoice in doing them good, and I will plant them in this land in faithfulness, *with all my heart and all my soul*" (Jer. 32:41 ESV).

Anger: "And when he had looked round about on them with anger, being grieved for the hardness of their hearts, he saith unto the man, Stretch forth thine hand. And he stretched it out: and his hand was restored whole as the other" (Mark 3:5 KJV).

Grief: "And it repented the LORD that he had made man on the earth, and it grieved him at his heart" (Gen. 6:6 KJV). "How often they rebelled against him in the wilderness and grieved him in the wasteland!" (Ps. 78:40 NIV).

Laughter:

> He that sitteth in the heavens shall laugh: the LORD shall have them in derision. (Ps. 2:4 KJV)

> The LORD shall laugh at him: for he seeth that his day is coming. (Ps. 37:13 KJV)

> I also will laugh at your calamity; I will mock when terror strikes you. (Prov. 1:26 ESV)

When we read these scriptures, it becomes clear that the heart is the harbor for all emotions. As I read about God's emotions, I found one that was absent—crying. I was basing my search on what I knew to be true as Jesus approached Jerusalem, "And when he drew near and saw the city, he wept over it" (Luke 19:41 NIV). I thought about the time that Lazarus died and how Christ was moved when he asked where Lazarus had been laid and "Jesus wept" (John 11:35), and he wept even though he knew he was going to raise him from the dead. He cried because he loved him. Then I realized the difference. Jesus was in the flesh and walking upon the earth. This is where we can see that God's emotions look closest to ours when we look at our redeemer clothed in flesh. God the father, who is a spirit, processes his emotions differently from the way we do. He exists outside of time so he can see circumstances not only as they presently are, but how they will turn out in the future. Sometimes our emotions overwhelm us but God does not have the element of uncertainty to deal with. He is never overwhelmed, for he is God. He possesses absolute clarity, and he is sovereign. God will use our purity in mind and in speech as an example to others. He will show his character through our integrity. He will care for others by our generosity. It is by our actions, word, and deed that we confirm our calling. "His divine power has granted to us all things that pertain to life and godliness, through the knowledge of him who called us to his own glory and excellence" (2 Pet 1:3 ESV).

The Spirit

Our will, our intellect, and our emotions need to be led by the Holy Spirit and how it lives in this world. The part of us that has spiritual discernment, where we get peace, and the part of us that communicates with God. This is where the Holy Spirit dwells within us.

In our journey to seek the truth, we will see that we are all "spiritually dead" when we are born. We will discover that we only come alive spiritually when we accept Christ, and we are born again. Babies and little children cannot sin even though we are all born into sin. Children have not developed mentally enough to determine what true sin is or how to interpret it or the knowledge on how to obtain salvation. They are pure in heart; therefore, they are blameless before God.

> "And when Jesus had cried with a loud voice, he said, Father, into thy hands I commend my spirit: and having said thus, he gave up the ghost." [Notice he did not ask God to receive his soul, but his spirit.] (Luke 23:46 KJV)

> And as they were stoning Stephen, he called out, "Lord Jesus, receive my spirit." And falling to his knees he cried out with a loud voice, "Lord, do not hold this sin against them." And when he had said this, he fell asleep. [Again Stephen asks Jesus to receive his spirit, not his soul.] (Acts 7:59–60 ESV)

> The natural person does not accept the things of the Spirit of God, for they are folly to him, and he is not able to understand them

because they are spiritually discerned. [In verse 7 the hidden wisdom of God is mentioned and states this wisdom was created by God before time itself.] (1 Cor. 2:14 ESV)

A new heart also will I give you, and a new spirit will I put within you: and I will take away the stony heart out of your flesh, and I will give you a heart of flesh. [God was speaking to his people that had lost their devotion to him and went among those that worshiped idols and God was concerned about the use of his holy name so he brought them out of other countries back to their land he told them he would give them "his spirit."] (Ezek. 36:26 KJV)

And afterward, I will pour out my Spirit on all people. Your sons and daughters will prophesy, your old men will dream dreams, your young men will see visions. [God is restoring Israel in this chapter of Joel and says he would again pour out "his spirit" upon them.] (Joel 2:28 NIV)

You know that your body is a sanctuary of the Holy Spirit who is in you, whom you have received from God, don't you? You do not belong to yourselves. (1 Cor. 6:19 ISV)

That which is born of the flesh is flesh, and that which is born of the Spirit is spirit. Marvel not that I said unto thee, Ye must be born again. (John 3:6–8 KJV)

For as the body apart from the spirit is dead, so also faith apart from works is dead. [This verse again tells us that if the spirit is absent from our bodies, then we are indeed departed. We also see the power of parallel and dual importance made again to where the joining of faith and works is an absolute necessity. One cannot endure without the other.] (James 2:26 ESV)

It is the Spirit who gives life; the flesh is no help at all. The words that I have spoken to you are spirit and life. [This is another dual comparison from the Word of God confirming that the spirit gives life. We know the life being represented here is eternal life. We know that biologically our blood gives the flesh its life.] (John 6:63 ESV)

Flesh gives birth to flesh, but the Spirit gives birth to spirit. You should not be surprised at my saying, "You must be born again. The wind blows wherever it pleases. You hear its sound, but you cannot tell where it comes from or where it is going. So it is with everyone born of the Spirit." (John 3:6–8 NIV)

And they fell on their faces and said, "O God, the God of the spirits of all flesh, shall one man sin, and will you be angry with all the congregation?" (Num. 16:22 ESV)

We can reach a factual conclusion that although the soul and the spirit are interchangeable, according to the scriptures, they hold different attributes distinct from one another, yet they are one. Just as God the father, Jesus the son of God, and the Holy Spirit of God are different, yet they are the same person. Three in one.

CHAPTER 2

The Significance of Biblical Numerology

The significance of biblical numerology became profound as I studied the way they constantly appear in the Bible with a significant meaning. There is a resounding reoccurrence of these numbers with familiar similarity in the complex mathematics and the laws that govern the cosmos and mankind. There is a vast universe of clues that God has left embedded in his word. They are scattered everywhere, if you should desire to find them. I think many of us familiar with the scriptures are unaware of these clear and distinct clues. I would suggest we need to put on a different pair of glasses so our vision becomes clear as we pray for renewed spiritual wisdom and awakening. The indifference and opposition to the Word of God are not without reasoning at all. You see, the Bible strips us of all our pride and the illusion of a masquerade that we all try to wear. It reveals our sin and reduces our wisdom to the ashes of speculation and therefore man's wisdom is discounted. Just as God describes his people as stiff-necked people so are, we all. God reveals our true condition and our depraved condition. All the genius mankind has mustered is mere child's play against the creator of wisdom itself. No depth of philosophy can deny him nor lose one stone of truth at its foundation. Archeologists and science have made great attempts to find sources of their theories, and they have plundered the very belly of the earth, only to discover with each shovel overturned their theories give way to the truth and accuracy of God's Word. God's Word is like a great anvil of truth, and many hammers of disbelief and skepticism lay broken all around it. The Bible is the Word of God, and it shows us a brief reflection of ourselves. Everything man creates, man can change, edit, or even destroy it. But what God has placed in motion, no man can put asunder nor change it.

Numerology by Coincidence or by Design?

God's Word and his works are never by coincidence. Only by his will or by his design. His ways are perfect. "As for God, his way is perfect: The LORD's word is flawless; he shields all who take refuge in him" (Ps. 18:30 NIV). It is in his perfect divine order the heavens and all things were made. "All things were made by him, and without him was not anything made that was made" (John 1:3 KJV). God has shown through his works that through the numeric scheme of things that everything has a purpose. The reason I wanted to explore numerology in the Bible was to see how the King of kings used numbers. The Bible itself was written by men from every diverse background imaginable. Shepherds, rich men, poor men, preachers, judges, and physicians. Men exiled to distant shores to a herdsman of flocks. Yet these men were hundreds of miles from one another, separated by both time and space. It took fifteen hundred years to write it, and the man who wrote the last page did not know of the one that wrote the first page. How is it that these men wrote in perfect harmony with each other and of one accord? "All Scripture is breathed out by God and profitable for teaching, for reproof, for correction, and training in righteousness" (2 Tim. 3:16 ESV), and again in 2 Peter 1:21, "For the prophecy came not in old time by the will of man: but holy men of God spake as they were moved by the Holy Ghost" (KJV).

The Number 3

The number 3 is used *467* times in the Bible. It is the symbol of completeness. This solidity and completeness suggest the Trinity of God, so three is a divine testimony or manifestation. This manifestation is sometimes in the resurrection of things moral, physical, and spiritual. Three is also the symbol of resurrection. The laws that govern the planets and the cosmos govern man as well. There are in measurement three dimensions, length, width, and thickness. These three are necessary to make up a solid. Three again is the symbol of completeness. God created time for us to live and have our very existence in a cycle of three. The present, the past, and the future. Although we cannot feel it, the earth itself is in motion three different ways all occurring at the same time. The earth *spins* on its axis, just as a top spins on its spindle. This spinning movement is called the Earth's *rotation*. While the earth spins on its axis, it also *orbits* or revolves around the sun. This movement is called *revolution*. There are three attributes of God—omniscience, omnipotence, and omnipresence.

"And the LORD appointed a great fish to swallow up Jonah. And Jonah was in the belly of the fish *three days* and *three nights*" (Jonah 1:17 ESV). Jonah had disobeyed God and there were violent storms and chaos so bad on the ship he was on he told them to cast him overboard because he was the reason for the storm.

"And immediately the rooster crowed a second time. And Peter remembered how Jesus had said to him, 'Before the rooster crows twice, you will deny me *three times*. And he broke down and wept" (Mark 14:72 ESV).

"Above it stood the seraphims: each one had six wings; with twain he covered his face, and with twain he covered his feet, and with twain he did fly. And one cried unto another, and said, Holy, holy, holy, is the LORD of hosts: the whole earth is full of his glory" (Isa. 6:2–3 KJV). The Seraphims called out holy *three times*. This was a vision Isaiah had in the year that King Uzziah died.

"Now when Daniel knew that the writing was signed, he went into his house; and his windows being open in his chamber toward

Jerusalem, he kneeled upon his knees *three times* a day, and prayed, and gave thanks before his God, as he did aforetime" (Dan. 6:10 KJV). Daniel was faithful to God, and in this chapter, the time was nearing when King Darius would have him placed into the lion's den where an angel would come and lock the jaws of the beasts so that he was not harmed.

"For there are *three that bear record in heaven*, the Father, the Word, and the Holy Ghost: and these *three are one*. And there are *three that bear witness in earth*, the Spirit, and the water, and the blood: and *these three agree in one*" (1 John 5:7–8 KJV).

"For all that is in the world he desires of the flesh and the desires of the eyes and pride of life[is not from the Father but is from the world" (1 John 2:16). These three are referred to as the completeness of temptation.

"The angel who was talking to me had a gold measuring rod to measure the city, its gates, and its walls. The city was cubic in shape: its length was the same as its width. He measured the city with his rod, and it measured at 12,000 stadia: Its length, width, and height were the same" (Rev. 21:14–16 NIV). The vision of the New Jerusalem coming down out of heaven was designed like a cube and the *three standards* of measurements we use today. The 12,000 referring to one Roman Sadion was 640 feet long so this would make the New Jerusalem 1,454 miles long.

"When they had finished eating, Jesus said to Simon Peter, 'Simon son of John, do you love me more than these?' 'Yes, Lord,' he said, 'you know that I love you.' Jesus said, 'Feed my lambs.' Again Jesus said, 'Simon son of John, do you love me?' He answered, 'Yes, Lord, you know that I love you.' Jesus said, 'Take care of my sheep'" (John 21:15–17 NIV).

The third time he said to him, "Simon son of John, do you love me?" Peter was hurt because Jesus asked him the third time, "Do you love me?" He said, "Lord, you know all things; you know that I love you." Jesus said, "Feed my sheep." Jesus asks Peter if he loves him *three times* and each time Peter answers yes, he tells him to feed his sheep.

"So, leaving them again, he went away and prayed for the *third time*, saying the same words again. Then he came to the disciples and said to them, 'Sleep and take your rest later. See, the hour is at hand, and the Son of Man is betrayed into the hands of sinners. Rise, let us be going; see, my betrayer is at hand'" (Matt. 26:44–46 (ESV). Jesus prayed three times before his arrest.

"And it was the third hour, and they crucified him" (Mark 15:25 KJV). The Lord was placed on the cross and crucified at the third hour of the day, which was 9:00 a.m.

"Now from the sixth hour there was darkness over all the land unto the ninth hour" (Matt. 27:45 KJV). Three hours after they placed Jesus on the Cross until from the six hour until the fourth hour or for three hours while he suffered there was darkness over the land.

"And about the ninth hour Jesus cried with a loud voice, saying, Eli, Eli, lama sabachthani? that is to say, My God, my God, why hast thou forsaken me? Some of them that stood there, when they heard that, said, This man calleth for Elias. And straightway one of them ran, and took a spunge, and filled it with vinegar, and put it on a reed, and gave him to drink. The rest said, Let be, let us see whether Elias will come to save him. Jesus, when he had cried again with a loud voice, yielded up the ghost" (Matt. 27:46–50 KJV). Jesus died on the ninth hour of the day or 3:00 p.m. He hung on that cross for you and me from 9:00 a.m. to 3:00 p.m. before he died. Six agonizing hours. It is not a mistake that 6 is the number of man.

On the first day of the week, very early in the morning, the women took the spices they had prepared and went to the tomb. They found the stone rolled away from the tomb, but when they entered, they did not find the body of the Lord Jesus. While they were wondering about this, suddenly two men in clothes that gleamed like lightning stood beside them. In their fright the women bowed down with their faces to the ground, but the men said to them, "Why do you

> look for the living among the dead? He is not
> here; he has risen! Remember how he told you,
> while he was still with you in Galilee: 'The Son of
> Man must be delivered over to the hands of sin-
> ners, be crucified and on the third day be raised
> again.' "Then they remembered his words."
> (Luke 24:1–8 NIV)

Jesus Christ, the son of both God and man, was buried on Friday and on the first day of the week on Sunday he arose.

"I am the God of Abraham, the God of Isaac, and the God of Jacob? He Is not the God of the dead but of the living" (Matt. 22:32 NIV). Abraham, Isaac, and Jacob, the *three* patriarchs.

"On coming to the house, they saw the child with his mother Mary, and they bowed down and worshiped him. Then they opened their treasures and presented him with gifts of gold, frankincense and myrrh" (Matt. 2:11). There is an absolute conclusion that there are three gifts brought to give to Jesus as stated in the gospel of Matthew. However, the Bible itself gives no definitive proof of three kings or Magi.

Jesus raised *three* people from the dead as recorded in the three scriptures that follow.

> Taking her by the hand he said to her,
> "Talitha cumi," which means, "Little girl, I say
> to you, arise." And immediately the girl got up
> and began walking (for she was twelve years of
> age), and they were immediately overcome with
> amazement. (Mark 5:41–42 ESV)

> Then he came up and touched the bier, and
> the bearers stood still. And he said, "Young man,
> I say to you, arise." And the dead man sat up and
> began to speak, and Jesus gave him to his mother.
> (Luke 7:14–15 ESV)

"So they took away the stone. Then Jesus looked up and said, "Father, I thank you that you have heard me. I knew that you always hear me, but I said this for the benefit of the people standing here, that they may believe that you sent me." When he had said this, Jesus called in a loud voice, "Lazarus, come out!" The dead man came out, his hands and feet wrapped with strips of linen, and a cloth around his face. Jesus said to them, "Take off the grave clothes and let him go." (John 11:41–44 NIV)

The Number 4

The number four appears 305 times in the Bible. It is the number of the four corners of the earth. The number four speaks of earthly completeness and universality.

And God said, "Let there be lights in the expanse of the heavens to separate the day from the night. And let them be for signs and for seasons, and for days and years, and let them be lights in the expanse of the heavens to give light upon the earth." And it was so. And God made the two great lights—the greater light to rule the day and the lesser light to rule the night—and the stars. And God set them in the expanse of the heavens to give light on the earth, to rule over the day and over the night, and to separate the light from the darkness. And God saw that it was good. And there was evening and there was morning, the fourth day." (Gen. 1:14–19 ESV)

On the fourth day of creation week, God completed the material universe. On this day, he brought into existence our sun, the moon, and all the stars. Their purpose was to give light and to divide the day from the night on earth. These elements gave mankind a demarcation of time. This system of dividing day from the night would give us what we measure and call time.

Eve, the woman that was made from Adam for Adam by God is mentioned only *four times* in the Bible in the scriptures that follow.

> And Adam called his wife's name Eve; because she was the mother of all living. (Gen. 3:20 KJV)

> And Adam knew Eve his wife; and she conceived, and bare Cain, and said, I have gotten a man from the LORD. (Gen. 4:1)

> But I fear, lest by any means, as the serpent beguiled Eve through his subtilty, so your minds should be corrupted from the simplicity that is in Christ. (2 Cor. 11:3 KJV)

> For Adam was first formed, then Eve. (1 Tim. 2:13 KJV)

If you look at the entire story's narrative between Satan and Eve in Genesis chapter 3, you will make two discoveries. First, Eve is not referred to by her name Eve, only by "woman." The second discovery is that Satan didn't wait for Eve to be alone because we read in Genesis 3:6 (NIV), "When the woman saw that the fruit of the tree was good for food and pleasing to the eye, and also desirable for gaining wisdom, she took some and ate it." She also gave some to her husband, *who was with her*, and he ate it. I basically reference three versions of the scriptures which are the *ESV*, *KJV*, and the *NIV*. All three versions plainly state Adam was by her side.

> I was amazed to see a wind storm blow in from the north, consisting of a massive cloud

> and fire that was flashing back and forth, sur-
> rounded by bright light. From deep within the
> cloud, something was shining that appeared to
> have a color like bronze that had been placed in
> fire until it glowed. Deep inside it, the likenesses
> of *four* living beings were visible. Their appear-
> ances were similar to human forms, except that
> they each had *four faces, four pairs of wings*, and
> straight legs. Their feet resembled calves' hooves,
> but they gleamed like polished bronze. From
> under their wings there were human hands on
> their *four sides*. Now as to their *four faces* and *four
> pairs of wings, their pairs of wings* overlapped each
> other. They moved in straight directions without
> turning their faces around as they moved. The
> form of their faces was human, but each of the
> four also had the face of a lion to the right, the
> face of an ox to the left, and the face of an eagle
> behind them. (Ezek. 1:4–10 ISV)

Ezekiel was a prisoner at the time of this great vision as he states in Ezekiel 1:1, "Now it came to pass in the thirtieth year, in the fourth month, on the fifth day of the month, as I was among the captives by the River Chebar, that the heavens were opened and I saw visions of God." According to Numbers 4:3, priests normally began their temple service in their thirtieth year. "From thirty years old up to fifty years old, all who can come on duty, to do the work in the tent of meeting" (ESV). Since Ezekiel was a Levite, the law of thirty applies as it pertains to priests.

Matthew, Mark, Luke, and John are the *four gospel accounts* of the life of Jesus and his ministry. Each gospel at times talks about a certain chain of events with a different narrative. However, each gospel emphasizes a special focus on the ministry of Christ.

The *four witnesses* of God on earth are miracles, wonders, signs, and the gifts of the Holy Spirit "God also testified to it by signs, wonders and various miracles, and by gifts of the Holy Spirit distributed according to his will" (Heb. 2:4 NIV).

The garden of Eden had a river that parted into the headwaters of *four other rivers.*

> A river watering the garden flowed from Eden; from there it was separated into four head-waters. The name of the first is Pishon; it winds through the entire land of Havilah, where there is gold. The gold of that land is good; aromatic resin and onyx are also there. The name of the second rive is Gihon; it winds through the entire land of Cush. The name of the third rive is the Tigris; it runs along the east side of Ashur. And the fourth river is the Euphrates. (Gen. 2:10–14 NIV)

After Jesus was crucified, his clothes were shared by soldiers. "Then the soldiers, when they had crucified Jesus, took his garments, and made *four parts*, to every soldier a part; and also his coat: now the coat was without seam, woven from the top throughout" (John 19:23 KJV).

Rainbows are mentioned *four times* in the scriptures.

> I do set my bow in the cloud, and it shall be for a token of a covenant between me and the earth. (Gen. 9:13 KJV)

> Like the appearance of the bow that is in the cloud on the day of rain, so was the appearance of the brightness all around. (Ezek. 1:28 ESV)

> And he who sat there had the appearance of jasper and carnelian, and around the throne was a rainbow that had the appearance of an emerald. (Rev. 4:3 ESV)

> Then I saw another mighty angel coming
> down from heaven, wrapped in a cloud, with a
> rainbow over his head, and his face was like the
> sun, and his legs like pillars of fire. (Rev. 10:1
> KJV)

There are *four* major cardinal points on the earth: east, north, south, and west. "There were three gates on the east, three on the north, three on the south and three on the west" (Rev. 21:13 NIV).

When God gave instructions for constructing an altar, he instructed the priests to construct an altar that has *four corners and four pillars*. Today, altars are still constructed with four corners and four pillars, which is a representation of the completeness of God. "You shall make the altar of acacia wood, five cubits long and five cubits broad. The alter shall be square, and its height shall be three cubits. And you shall make horns for it on its *four corners*; its horns shall be of one piece with it and you shall overlay it with bronze" (Exod. 27:1–2).

The Number 7

Several numbers are repeated many times in the scripture, and again, it is no coincidence that these same numbers relate to our material world and to everything God has created. The number 7 is used 735 times in the Bible. The number 7 is the foundation of God's Word. Seven is the number of completeness and perfection both physical and spiritual. It is also a day that represents holy.

"And the words of the Lord are flawless, like silver purified in a crucible, like gold refined seven times" (Ps. 12:6 NIV).

"For in six days the LORD made heaven and earth, the sea, and all that is in them, and rested on the seventh day. Therefore the LORD blessed the Sabbath day and made it holy" (ESV). So God from the beginning as marked the seventh day as divine and holy.

In Matthew 13, Jesus gives seven parables and seven psalms are ascribed to David in the New Testament, which are Psalms 2, 16, 32, 41, 69, 95, and 109.

Jesus performed seven miracles on God's holy Sabbath Day. Each of these seven miracles is recorded in Mark 1:29–31, Mark 3:1–6, Mark 1:21–28, Luke 13:10–17, Luke 14:1–6, and John 5:1–18.

Jesus healed the withered hand of a man who was in the synagogue services.

> Going on from that place, he went into their synagogue, and a man with a shriveled hand was there. Looking for a reason to bring charges against Jesus, they asked him, "Is it lawful to heal on the Sabbath?" He said to them, "If any of you has a sheep and it falls into a pit on the Sabbath, will you not take hold of it and lift it out? How much more valuable is a person than a sheep! Therefore it is lawful to do good on the Sabbath? Then he said to the man, "Stretch out your hand." So he stretched it out and it was completely restored, just as sound as the other. (Matt. 12:9–13 NIV)

> At a Capernaum synagogue, he casts out an unclean spirit that possessed a man who cried out. "They went to Capernaum, and when the Sabbath came, Jesus went into the synagogue and began to teach. The people were amazed at his teaching because he taught them as ones who had authority, not as the teachers of the law. Just then a man in their synagogue who was possessed by an impure spirit cried out, "What do you want with us, Jesus of Nazareth? Have you come to destroy us? I know who you are-the Holy One of God!" "Be quiet!" said Jesus sternly. "Come out of him!" The impure spirit shook the man vio-

lently and came out of him with a shriek. (Mark
1:21–26 NIV)

Right after the above miracle, Jesus heals Peter's wife's mother
of fever and that evening heals many more, all on the Holy Day of
the Sabbath.

> And immediately he left the synagogue and
> entered the house of Simon and Andrew, with
> James and John. Now Simon's mother-in-law lay
> ill with a fever, and immediately they told him
> about her. And he came and took her by the
> hand and lifted her up, and the fever left her, and
> she began to serve them. That evening at sun-
> down they brought to him all who were sick or
> oppressed by demons. And the whole city was
> gathered at the door. And he healed many who
> were sick with various diseases and cast out many
> demons. And he would not permit the demons
> to speak, because they knew him. (Mark 1:29–34
> ESV)

A woman attending synagogue, who was made sick by a demon
for eighteen years, is released from her bondage.

> And there was a woman who had had a
> disabling spirit for eighteen years. She was bent
> over and could not fully straighten herself. When
> Jesus saw her, he called her over and said to her,
> "Woman, you are freed from your disability.
> "And he laid his hands on her, and immediately
> she was made straight, and she glorified God. But
> the ruler of the synagogue, indignant because
> Jesus had healed on the Sabbath, said to the peo-
> ple, "There are six days in which work ought to
> be done. Come on those days and be healed, and

not on the Sabbath day." Then the Lord answered him, "You hypocrites! Does not each of you on the Sabbath untie his ox or his donkey from the manger and lead it away to water it? And ought not this woman, a daughter of Abraham whom Satan bound for eighteen years, be loosed from this bond on the Sabbath day?" (Luke 13:11–16 ESV)

In these scriptures, God's Word reveals to us the true source of disease and maladies. It is Satan. It is not a test; it is the work of Satan when one of our loved ones becomes afflicted with a disease, disability, or a condition.

At a Pharisee's house, eating a meal with the host and several lawyers, Jesus heals a man with dropsy.

And, behold, there was a certain man before him which had dropsy. And Jesus answering spake unto the lawyers and Pharisees, saying, Is it lawful to heal on the sabbath day? And they held their peace. And he took him, and healed him, and let him go; And answered them, saying, Which of you shall have an ass or an ox fell into a pit, and will not straightway pull him out on the sabbath day? And they could not answer him again to these things. (Luke 14:2–6 KJV)

A man who is disabled and unable to walk is healed at the pool of Bethesda.

When Jesus saw him lying there and knew that he had already been there a long time, he said to him, "Do you want to be healed?" The sick man answered him, "Sir, I have no one to put me into the pool when the water is stirred up, and while I am going another steps down before

> me "Jesus said to him, "Get up, take up your bed,
> and walk." And at once the man was healed, and
> he took up his bed and walked. Now that day was
> the Sabbath." (John 5:6–9 ESV)

Jesus heals a man born blind at the pool of Siloam.

> They brought to the Pharisees the man who
> had formerly been blind. Now it was a Sabbath
> day when Jesus made the mud and opened his
> eyes. So the Pharisees again asked him how he
> had received his sight. And he said to them, "He
> put mud on my eyes, and I washed, and I see."
> Some of the Pharisees said, "This man is not
> from God, for he does not keep the Sabbath."
> But others said, "How can a man who is a sinner
> do such signs?" And there was a division among
> them." (John 9:13–16)

The number 7 is used fifty-five times in the book of Revelations. Some of those are seven churches, seven angels to the seven churches, seven seals, seven trumpet plagues, seven thunders, and the seven last plagues. The first resurrection of the dead takes place at the seventh trumpet, completing salvation for the Church.

When Peter asked Christ about unforgiveness we read, "Then Peter came up and said to him, 'Lord, how often will my brother sin against me, and I forgive him? As many as seven times?' Jesus said to him, 'I do not say to you seven times, but seventy-seven times'" (Mat. 18:21–22 ESV).

Jesus performed seven miracles on God's holy Sabbath Day.

How do we relate to the number 7 in the physical world? It comes up everywhere. In colors, for example. You can pass light through a three-sided block of glass, and it is broken up into its component colors, which are seven in number, and form what is called the sun's spectrum. Each element radiates its special color, those seven colors of the spectrum point to the seven-fold fold composition of the sun itself. These same seven colors paint the beauty of the rainbow through water particles. According to geologists, the core of the earth is made up of seven basic layers, the core being volcanic by nature and pressed down by the pressure of water, or aqueous rock. Sound is the vibrations of air, whether in the wind that moves across the earth or through our larynx and air pressure to vibrate our vocal cords, the frequency of vibrations determining the pitch of the sound, whether low or high. For each note of the scale, the number of vibrations per second is a multiple of eleven, while the difference in the number of vibrations for each note is also a multiple of eleven. The scale itself consists of seven notes. If we look at biblical chronology the same numeric law prevails. That given by God to Israel was based upon the numeral seven. On the seventh day, they rested, in the seventh month were special feasts, in the seventh year, the land lay fallow, while the forty-ninth, seven times seven was the emancipation year or the year of jubilee.

By observing the laws of nature, we see the same system of arithmetic from the arrangement of plants in their leaves and division of flowers to animals that are partial among tribes and numbers. Heaven's arithmetic applies from here to infinity.

The Number 10

In the Bible, the number 10 is used 242 times. Ten is viewed as a complete and perfect number. The same is true of 3, 7, and 12. The number 10 is made up of 4, the number of the physical creation, and 6, the number of man. The number 10 signifies testimony, law, responsibility, and the completeness of order. In Genesis 1 we find the phrase "God said" ten times, which is a testimony of His creative power.

God gave the Ten Commandments to man.

> And God spoke all these words, saying, I am
> the Lord your God, who brought you out of the
> land of Egypt, out of the house of slavery. You

shall have no other gods before me. You shall not make for yourself a carved image, or any likeness of anything that is in heaven above, or that is in the earth beneath, or that is in the water under the earth. You shall not bow down to them or serve them, for I the LORD your God am a jealous God, visiting the iniquity of the fathers on the children to the third and the fourth generation of those who hate me, but showing steadfast love to thousands of those who love me and keep my commandments. You shall not take the name of the LORD your God in vain, for the LORD will not hold him guiltless who takes his name in vain. Remember the Sabbath day, to keep it holy. Six days you shall labor, and do all your work, but the seventh day is a Sabbath to the LORD your God. On it you shall not do any work, you, or your son, or your daughter, your male servant, or your female servant, or your livestock, or the sojourner who is within your gates. For in six days the LORD made heaven and earth, the sea, and all that is in them, and rested on the seventh day. Therefore the LORD blessed the Sabbath day and made it holy. Honor your father and your mother, that your days may be long in the land that the LORD your God is giving you. You shall not murder. You shall not commit adultery. You shall not steal. You shall not bear false witness against your neighbor. You shall not covet your neighbor's house; you shall not covet your neighbor's wife, or his male servant, or his female servant, or his ox, or his donkey, or anything that is your neighbor's. (Exod. 20:1–17 ESV)

The Passover lamb was selected on day 10 of the first month. "Tell all the congregation of Israel that on the tenth day of this month every man shall take a lamb according to their fathers' houses, a lamb for a household" (Exod. 12:3 ESV).

Day 10 of the seventh month is also the Holy Day known as the Day of Atonement. "Purge out therefore the old leaven, that ye may be a new lump, as ye are unleavened. For even Christ our passover is sacrificed for us" (1 Cor. 5:7 KJV).

Pagan Egypt experienced ten plagues from God, to release his people, which was also the reaction to human disobedience (Exod. 7:14–11:10).

The Number 12

Twelve can be found in 187 places in God's Word. Revelation contains twenty-two of those. The meaning of 12, which is considered a perfect number, is that it symbolizes God's power and authority, as well as serving as a perfect governmental foundation. It can also symbolize the completeness of the nation of Israel. Jacob (Israel) had twelve sons, each representing a tribe begun by a prince for a total of twelve princes. Ishmael born to Abraham through the maidservant Hagar also had twelve princes.

God specified that twelve unleavened cakes of bread be placed every week in the temple with frankincense next to each of the two piles that were to be made. The priests were commanded to change the bread every Sabbath day "And thou shalt take fine flour, and bake twelve cakes thereof: two tenth deals shall be in one cake" (Lev. 24:5 KJV).

Moses sent out twelve spies to explore Canaan.

> The LORD spoke to Moses, saying, "Send men to spy out the land of Canaan, which I am giving to the people of Israel. From each tribe of their fathers you shall send a man, every one a chief among them." So Moses sent them from the wilderness of Paran, according to the command of the LORD, all of them men who were heads of

the people of Israel. And these were their names:
From the tribe of Reuben, Shammua the son of
Zaccur; from the tribe of Simeon, Shaphat the son
of Hori; from the tribe of Judah, Caleb the son
of Jephunneh; from the tribe of Issachar, Igal the
son of Joseph; from the tribe of Ephraim, Hoshea
the son of Nun; from the tribe of Benjamin, Palti
the son of Raphu; from the tribe of Zebulun,
Gaddiel the son of Sodi; from the tribe of Joseph
(that is, from the tribe of Manasseh), Gaddi the
son of Susi; from the tribe of Dan, Ammiel the
son of Gemalli; from the tribe of Asher, Sethur
the son of Michael; from the tribe of Naphtali,
Nahbi the son of Vophsi; from the tribe of Gad,
Geuel the son of Machi. These were the names of
the men whom Moses sent to spy out the land.
And Moses called Hoshea the son of Nun Joshua.
Moses sent them to spy out the land of Canaan
and said to them, "Go up into the Negeb and go
up into the hill country, and see what the land
is, and whether the people who dwell in it are
strong or weak, whether they are few or many,
and whether the land that they dwell in is good
or bad, and whether the cities that they dwell in
are camps or strongholds, and whether the land
is rich or poor, and whether there are trees in it
or not. Be of good courage and bring some of the
fruit of the land." Now the time was the season of
the first ripe grapes. (Num. 13:1–20 ESV)

Christ chose twelve men to be his disciples and bear witness to his
ministry and preach the gospel.

And he goeth up into a mountain, and
calleth unto him whom he would: and they
came unto him. And he ordained twelve, that

they should be with him, and that he might send them forth to preach. And to have power to heal sicknesses, and to cast out devils: And Simon he surnamed Peter; And James the son of Zebedee, and John the brother of James; and he surnamed them Boanerges, which is, The sons of thunder: And Andrew, and Philip, and Bartholomew, and Matthew, and Thomas, and James the son of Alphaeus, and Thaddaeus, and Simon the Canaanite, And Judas Iscariot, which also betrayed him: and they went into an house. (Mark 3:13–19 KJV)

John had been exiled to the island of Patmos because he teaching Jesus Christ and him crucified. While on Patmos, God gave John a vision of the final days of earth, and a peek at heaven.

The number 12 is extremely symbolic in that vision.

Then I saw another angel ascending from the rising of the sun, with the seal of the living God, and he called with a loud voice to the four angels who had been given power to harm earth and sea, saying, "Do not harm the earth or the sea or the trees, until we have sealed the servants of our God on their foreheads." And I heard the number of the sealed, 144,000, sealed from every tribe of the sons of Israel: 12,000 from the tribe of Judah were sealed, 12,000 from the tribe of Reuben, 12,000 from the tribe of Gad, 12,000 from the tribe of Asher, 12,000 from the tribe of Naphtali, 12,000 from the tribe of Manasseh, 12,000 from the tribe of Simeon, 12,000 from the tribe of Levi, 12,000 from the tribe of Issachar, 12,000 from the tribe of Zebulun, 12,000 from the tribe of Joseph, 12,000 from the tribe of Benjamin were sealed. (Rev. 7:2–8 ESV)

Christ's bride, which is his church, wears a crown containing twelve stars. "And a great sign appeared in heaven: a woman clothed with the sun, with the moon under her feet, and on her head a crown of twelve stars" (Rev. 12:1 ESV).

In John's vision, he was shown the New Jerusalem. The use of 12 is very profound in the description. The description itself is beyond man's imagination.

> And he carried me away in the Spirit to a great, high mountain, and showed me the holy city Jerusalem coming down out of heaven from God, having the glory of God, its radiance like a most rare jewel, like a jasper, clear as crystal. It had a great, high wall, with twelve gates, and at the gates twelve angels, and on the gates the names of the twelve tribes of the sons of Israel were inscribed—on the east three gates, on the north three gates, on the south three gates, and on the west three gates. And the wall of the city had twelve foundations, and on them were the twelve names of the twelve apostles of the Lamb.
>
> And the one who spoke with me had a measuring rod of gold to measure the city and its gates and walls. The city lies foursquare, its length the same as its width. And he measured the city with his rod, 12,000 stadia. Its length and width and height are equal. He also measured its wall, 144 cubits by human measurement, which is also an angel's measurement. The wall was built of jasper, while the city was pure gold, like clear glass. The foundations of the wall of the city were adorned with every kind of jewel. The first was jasper, the second sapphire, the third agate, the fourth emerald, the fifth onyx, the sixth carnelian, the seventh chrysolite, the eighth beryl, the ninth topaz, the tenth chrysoprase, the eleventh jacinth, the

> twelfth amethyst. And the twelve gates were twelve pearls, each of the gates made of a single pearl, and the street of the city was pure gold, like transparent glass. (Rev. 21:10–21 ESV)

The twelve patriarchs from and including Shem who was one of Noah's son's to Jacob (Israel) are Shem, Arphaxad, Salah, Heber, Peleg, Reu, Serug, Nahor, Terah, Abraham, Isaac, and Jacob.

Solomon appointed twelve officers over Israel. "Solomon had twelve district governors over all Israel, who supplied provisions for the king and the royal household. Each one had to provide supplies for one month in the year" (1 King 4:7 NIV).

The high priest's breastplate, also called the breastplate of decision, had twelve stones embedded in it. "And the stones shall be with the names of the children of Israel, twelve, according to their names, like the engravings of a signet; every one with his name shall they be according to the twelve tribes" (Exod. 28:21 KJV).

Jesus heals a woman who had been bleeding for twelve years.

> And, behold, a woman, which was diseased with an issue of blood twelve years, came behind him, and touched the hem of his garment: For she said within herself, If I may but touch his garment, I shall be whole. But Jesus turned him about, and when he saw her, he said, Daughter, be of good comfort; thy faith hath made thee whole. And the woman was made whole from that hour. (Matt. 9:20–22 KJV)

Jesus first spoke in the temple with religious leaders at the age of twelve when he and his family had traveled to Jerusalem for Passover.

> Now his parents went to Jerusalem every year at the Feast of the Passover. And when he was twelve years old, they went up according to custom. And when the feast was ended, as they

were returning, the boy Jesus stayed behind in Jerusalem. His parents did not know it, but supposing him to be in the group they went a day's journey, but then they began to search for him among their relatives and acquaintances, and when they did not find him, they returned to Jerusalem, searching for him. After three days they found him in the temple, sitting among the teachers, listening to them and asking them questions. And all who heard him were amazed at his understanding and his answers. And when his parents saw him, they were astonished. And his mother said to him, "Son, why have you treated us so? Behold, your father and I have been searching for you in great distress." And he said to them, "Why were you looking for me? Did you not know that I must be in my Father's house? And they did not understand the saying that he spoke to them. And he went down with them and came to Nazareth and was submissive to them. And his mother treasured up all these things in her heart." (Luke 2:41–52 ESV)

When Nebuchadnezzar has a dream that is interpreted by Daniel as the King will behave like a wild beast and the dream is fulfilled 12 months later. "All this came upon King Nebuchadnezzar. At the end of twelve months he was walking on the roof of the royal palace of Babylon" (Dan. 4:28–29 ESV).

When Jesus performs the miracle of the feeding of the five thousand, the disciples gather twelve baskets full of leftovers.

Then he ordered the crowds to sit down on the grass, and taking the five loaves and the two fish, he looked up to heaven and said a blessing. Then he broke the loaves and gave them to the disciples, and the disciples gave them to the

> crowds. And they all ate and were satisfied. And
> they took up twelve baskets full of the broken
> pieces left over. (Matt. 14:19–20 ESV)

A tree of life will also be in the new world God brings at the end of time with twelve fruits, one for each month of the year.

> Then the angel showed me the river of the
> water of life, as clear as crystal, flowing from the
> throne of God and of the Lamb down the mid-
> dle of the great street of the city. On each side
> of the river stood the tree of life, bearing twelve
> crops of fruit, yielding its fruit every month. And
> the leaves of the tree are for the healing of the
> nations. (Rev. 22:1–2 NIV)

Twelve thousand men come to battle the Midianites in a thousand from each tribe. "You shall send a thousand from each of the tribes of Israel to the war." So there were provided, out of the thousands of Israel, a thousand from each tribe, twelve thousand armed for war (Num. 31:4–5 ESV).

Elisha is called into his prophetic ministry by Elijah while plowing with twelve oxen.

So he departed thence, and found Elisha the son of Shaphat, who was plowing with twelve yoke of oxen before him, and he with the twelfth: and Elijah passed by him, and cast his mantle upon him. And he left the oxen, and ran after Elijah, and said, Let me, I pray thee, kiss my father and my mother, and then I will follow thee. And he said unto him, Go back again: for what have I done to thee? (1 King 19:19–20 KJV)

Ezra sets apart twelve priests when Israel returns from captivity. "Then I set apart twelve of the leading priests, namely, Sherebiah, Hashabiah and ten of their brothers, and I weighed out to them the offering of silver and gold and the articles that the king, his advisers, his officials and all Israel present there had donated for the house of our God" (Ezra 8:24–25 NIV).

The Number 40

The number 40 appears 159 times in the scriptures It generally symbolizes testing, a trial, or probation. The numeral 40 has for its meaning trial. It is the period of full probation, of complete testing.

The Jewish people of Israel held the belief that manhood was attained at the age of forty.

For Moses, the different phases of his life were guided by the number 40. "When he was forty years old, it came into his heart to visit his brothers, the children of Israel" (Acts 7:23 ESV). Then for forty years kept the flocks in Midian Acts. "And when forty years were expired, there appeared to him in the wilderness of mount Sina an angel of the Lord in a flame of fire in a bush. "And when forty years were expired, there appeared to him in the wilderness of mount Sina an angel of the Lord in a flame of fire in a bush" (Acts 7:30 KJV). Again when he received the ten commandments from God the number 40 appears as prominent in his life once more. "So he was there with the LORD forty days and forty nights. He neither ate bread nor drank water. And he wrote on the tablets the words of the covenant, the Ten Commandments" (Exod. 34:28 ESV). For the last forty years of his life, he wandered in the desert with the disobedient children of Israel. "The people of Israel ate the manna forty years, till they came to a habitable land. They ate the manna till they came to the border of the land of Canaan" (Exod. 16:35 ESV). If you've followed the time frame of Moses's life it was exactly in increments of 40 in the three phases of his life and in between as well. "Moses was a hundred and twenty years old when he died, yet his eyes were not weak nor his strength gone" (Deut. 34:7 NIV).

God flooded the earth with water for forty days and forty nights. "And rain fell on the earth forty days and forty nights" (Gen. 7:12 NIV).

Jesus fasted in the desert and was tempted by Satan for forty days. "Then Jesus was led up by the Spirit into the wilderness to be tempted by the devil. And after fasting forty days and forty nights, he was hungry" (Matt. 4:1–2 ESV).

After his resurrection, Jesus walked the earth for forty days before ascending back to heaven.

King David ruled Israel for forty years. "David *was* thirty years old when he began to reign, *and* he reigned forty years" (2 Sam. 5:4 KJV). And his son King Solomon ruled over Israel for forty years. "And the time that Solomon reigned in Jerusalem over all Israel *was* forty years" (1 King 11:42 KJV).

Goliath taunted the army of Israel twice a day for forty days before David defeated him. "For forty days the Philistine came forward and took his stand, morning and evening" (1 Sam. 17:16 ESV).

The prophet Jonah powerfully warned ancient Nineveh, for forty days, that its destruction would come because of its many sins. "And Jonah began to enter the city on the first day's walk. Then he cried out and said, "Yet forty days, and Nineveh shall be overthrown!" (Jonah 3:4 KJV).

The prophet Ezekiel laid on his right side for forty days to symbolize Judah's sins. "And when you have completed these, you shall lie down a second time, but on your right side, and bear the punishment of the house of Judah. Forty days I assign you, a day for each year" (Ezek. 4:6 ESV).

Elijah went forty days without food or water on his journey to Mt. Horeb.

> And he lay down and slept under a broom tree. And behold, an angel touched him and said to him, "Arise and eat." And he looked, and behold, there was at his head a cake baked on hot stones and a jar of water. And he ate and drank and lay down again. And the angel of the LORD came again a second time and touched him and said, "Arise and eat, for the journey is too great for you." And he arose and ate and drank and went in the strength of that food forty days and forty nights to Horeb, the mount of God. (1 King 19:5–8 ESV)

Five of the fifteen judges governed according to God's will for forty years. They were Othniel, Deborah and Barak, Eli and Gideon. Although not kings of Israel, they represented God and were inspired to execute his will (Judges 3:9–11, Judges 4:1–23, 1 Sam. 1:1–4:18, Judges 8:28).

Both Isaac and Esau were forty years old when they were first married. "And Isaac was forty years old when he married Rebekah daughter of Bethuel the Aramean from Paddan Aram and sister of Laban the Aramean" (Gen. 25:20 NIV). Remember, Jewish culture felt that manhood is attained at the age of forty.

"When Esau was forty years old, he married Judith, daughter of Beeri the Hittite, and also Basemath daughter of Elon the Hittite" (Gen. 26:34 NIV).

Abraham tried to bargain with God to not destroy Sodom and Gomorrah if forty righteous people were found in Genesis. "And he spoke to Him yet again and said, "Suppose there should be forty found there?" So He said, "I will not do it for the sake of forty" (Gen. 18:29 KJV).

Forty people wrote the Bible. Most of them we know, but there are anonymous writers too. Some of the authors wrote one book while some wrote several. Let me share the information.

Moses is credited for the first five books of the Old Testament: Genesis, Exodus, Leviticus, Numbers, and Deuteronomy, which are called the Pentateuch. These books cover creation to his death at the end of Deuteronomy. It's been suggested that another person, who took over the spiritual leadership of the Israelites, completed Deuteronomy.

The books of Joshua, Judges, and Ruth are historical documents written before or during the reign of King David presumably by priestly historians.

The psalms were written by King David, Moses, Solomon, the sons of Korah, the sons of Asaph, and Ethan the Ezrahite. Some Psalms were written anonymously.

Proverbs, Song of Solomon, and Ecclesiastes were written by King Solomon, though chapters 30 and 31 of Proverbs were written by Agur and Lemuel respectively.

Isaiah, Hosea, Amos, Jonah, Micah, Nahum, and Zephaniah were the prophets who penned the books with their names.

The writers of Samuel, Kings, Esther, and Job are unnamed.

Habakkuk, Joel, Obadiah, Ezekiel, Daniel, Haggai, Zechariah, and Malachi were written by the prophets' names respectively.

Jeremiah wrote both Lamentations and Jeremiah while Ezra wrote Ezra, Nehemiah, and possibly Chronicles.

In the New Testament, Matthew, Mark, Luke, and John wrote their gospels and Luke also wrote the book of Acts. Paul is responsible for the Pauline Letters which are Romans, 1 Corinthians, 2 Corinthians, Galatians, Ephesians, Philippians, Colossians, 1 Thessalonians, 2 Thessalonians, 1 Timothy, 2 Timothy, Titus, and Philemon.

Peter of the twelve disciples wrote 1 and 2 Peter. John, the disciple that Jesus loved, wrote 1, 2, and 3 John and also Revelation.

The book of James has been credited to James the brother of Jesus, and the book of Jude was written by Jude the brother of Jesus and James. Hebrews has been ascribed to the Apostle Paul but is generally considered to have been written anonymously.

The spies searched the land of Canaan for forty days. "At the end of forty days they returned from exploring the land" (Num. 13:25 NIV).

Forty lashes were the maximum whipping penalty. "Forty stripes may be given him, but not more, lest, if one should go on to beat him with more stripes than these, your brother be degraded in your sight" (Deut. 25:3 ESV).

God allowed the land to rest for forty years. "And the land had rest forty years. And Othniel the son of Kenaz died" (Judges 3:11 KJV).

Abdon, a judge in Israel, had forty sons, judges. "He had forty sons and thirty grandsons, who rode on seventy donkeys, and he judged Israel eight years" (Judges 12:14 ESV).

Israel did evil; God gave them to an enemy for forty years. "And the people of Israel again did what was evil in the sight of the LORD, so the LORD gave them into the hand of the Philistines for forty years" (Judges 13:1 ESV).

Ish-bosheth, Saul's son, was forty years old when he began to reign. "Ish-Bosheth son of Saul was forty years old when he became king over Israel, and he reigned two years. The tribe of Judah, however, remained loyal to David" (2 Samuel 2:10 NIV).

The holy place of the temple was forty cubits long. "The house, that is, the nave in front of the inner sanctuary, was forty cubits long" (1 Kings 6:17 ESV).

Joash reigned forty years in Jerusalem. "In the seventh year of Jehu, Joash became king, and he reigned in Jerusalem forty years. His mother's name was Zibiah; she was from Beersheba" (2 Kings 12:1 KJV).

Egypt to be laid desolate for forty years.

> The foot of neither man nor beast will pass through it; no one will live there for forty years. I will make the land of Egypt desolate among devastated lands, and her cities will lie desolate forty years among ruined cities. And I will disperse the Egyptians among the nations and scatter them through the countries. (Ezek. 29:11–12 NIV)

CHAPTER 3

Time Frame from Adam to the Flood

We could say that Adam was born in the year zero. I do not want to entertain the question of how many years did Adam live before he and Eve sinned. Instead, I am going to select what God's Word states in simple language. I do not want to go by how many generations passed between Adam and Noah because that tends to be muddy waters as well.

"And all the days that Adam lived were nine hundred and thirty years: and he died" (Gen. 5:5 KJV). So we know this is a fact. God does not have to subtract the beginning of Adam from the time that Adam sinned to get an accurate number. His word speaks to this question directly.

Noah was born in the year 1056. If we take the year of Noah's birth 1056 and subtract the years of Adam's life who was born in the year zero then you get 1056 – 930 = 126. Noah was born 126 years after Adam died. The great flood came when Noah was 600 years old. "And Noah was six hundred years old when the flood of waters was upon the earth" (Gen. 7:6 KJV).

Therefore, Adam lived to be 930 years old plus Noah was born 126 years later. Let's add 930 years + 126 years = 1,056. Remember Noah "was born" 126 years after Adam died and we know Noah was 600 years old when the great flood came so we add that 1,056 and Noah's age of 600 years when the flood came and that calculates to 1,656 years. This is exactly what God says in his word. We just must do some subtraction and addition. The final calculation is that the world existed 1,656 years before the great flood.

Did Methuselah Die in the Great Flood?

"When Methuselah had lived 187 years, he fathered Lamech" (Gen. 5:25 ESV).

According to Genesis 5, Methuselah was 187 when he had Lamech who was 182 when he had Noah. So that would make Methuselah 369 when his grandson Noah was born. "In the six hundredth year of Noah's life, in the second month, the seventeenth day of the month, the same day were all the fountains of the great deep broken up, and the windows of heaven were opened" (Gen. 7:11 KJV). The scriptures tell us that Noah was 600 when the waters came, so you get 969 as the age of Methuselah in the year of the flood. Therefore, he died in the year of the great flood. We are not told that he died as a result of the flood. God is silent with any further details. I want to just add a personal observation. Methuselah was the son of Enoch. The scriptures tell us that Enoch was 65 years old when Methuselah was born. After Methuselah was born, Enoch walked with God 300 years more, then God took him without him dying a physical death. I have wondered since Enoch was so close to God was that why God blessed Methuselah with such a long life?

Where Do We Go When We Die?

Where do we go when we die, or do we just cease to exist? As we explore probably one of the most asked questions of all times it is important to note that when death is spoken of it is the death of the body. There are times when someone dies referred to as being asleep. I begin with 2 Corinthians 5:8 extending what three different versions of the Bible (KJV, ESV, and NIV) say. This is one of the most controversial verses in God's Word.

From 2 Corinthians 5:8, "We are confident, I say, and willing rather to be absent from the body, and to be present with the Lord" (KJV). The ESV reads, "Yes, we are of good courage, and we would rather be away from the body and at home with the Lord." The NIV reads, "We are confident, I say, and would prefer to be away from the body and at home with the Lord." All three versions of the Bible are stating a preference which is "rather to be" and "prefer to be." These are not statements of fact that when we die, we immediately go to heaven.

"Then said his disciples, Lord, if he sleep, he shall do well. Howbeit Jesus spake of his death: but they thought that he had spoken of taking of rest in sleep. Then said Jesus unto them plainly, Lazarus is dead" (John 11:12–14). In this verse, Jesus strikes a difference between being physically asleep and being dead.

"By the sweat of your face you shall eat bread, till you return to the ground, for out of it you were taken; for you are dust, and to dust you shall return" (Genesis 3:19). This verse confirms we (our bodies) will return to the earth from where it came.

From 1 John 3:2:

> Beloved, we are God's children now, and what we will be has not yet appeared; but we know that when he appears we shall be like him, because we shall see him as he is. (ESV)

> Beloved, now are we the sons of God, and it doth not yet appear what we shall be: but we know that, when he shall appear, we shall be like him; for we shall see him as he is. (KJV)

> Dear friends, now we are children of God, and what we will be has not yet been made known. But we know that when Christ appears, we shall be like him, for we shall see him as he is. (NIV)

A "glorified body" will not be reunited with the spirit until Jesus returns. It does not matter whether our earthly remains have been cremated, buried, or lost at sea. Nothing is impossible for God. "All things were made through him, and without him was not anything made that was made" (John 1:3).

Then he said, "Jesus, remember me when you come into your kingdom. "Jesus answered him, "Truly I tell you, today you will be with me in paradise" (Luke 23:42–43). The scripture is plain here and no interpretation is needed. Jesus and the thief went to paradise, not to heaven.

"Jesus saith unto her, Touch me not; for I am not yet ascended to my Father: but go to my brethren, and say unto them, I ascend unto my Father, and your Father; and to my God, and your God" (John 20:17). John 20:17 confirms that when Jesus arose from the dead after three days he had not been to heaven.

> Let not your heart be troubled: ye believe in God, believe also in me. In my Father's house are many mansions: if it were not so, I would have told you. I go to prepare a place for you. And if I go and prepare a place for you, I will come again, and receive you unto myself; that where I am, there ye may be also. (John 14:1–3)

Jesus tells his disciples that he is going to prepare a place for them. Since he has not returned yet we know that Christ is still preparing a place for all that remain faithful to their end or to the time of his return. Heaven simply is a grand work in progress. The grandeur of it is hard to imagine and beyond our comprehension. Remember the Bible only speaks of two human beings that we can say are in heaven and both without tasting death because God says so.

Of course, the two I am speaking of are Enoch and Elijah.

CHAPTER 4

Did Magic and Wizards Exist in Biblical Times?

Yes, they of these and them some existed and are spoken about in both the Old and New Testaments. God has made it clear that to practice such things is an abomination to him. The occult is real and it is something that should not be toyed with. It is important that we not confuse the power of God with such things.

> When you come into the land that the LORD your God is giving you, you shall not learn to follow the abominable practices of those nations. There shall not be found among you anyone who burns his son or his daughter as an offering, anyone who practices divination or tells fortunes or interprets omens, or a sorcerer or a charmer or a medium or a necromancer or one who inquires of the dead, for whoever does these things is an abomination to the LORD. And because of these abominations the LORD your God is driving them out before you. (Deut. 18:9–12 ESV)

> And this became known to all the residents of Ephesus, both Jews, and Greeks. And fear fell

upon them all, and the name of the Lord Jesus was extolled. Also, many of those who were now believers came, confessing and divulging their practices. And a number of those who had practiced magic arts brought their books together and burned them in the sight of all. And they counted the value of them and found it came to fifty thousand pieces of silver. (Acts 19:17–19 ESV)

A man also or woman that hath a familiar spirit, or that is a wizard, shall surely be put to death: they shall stone them with stones: their blood shall be upon them. (Lev. 20:27 KJV)

And when they shall say unto you, Seek unto them that have familiar spirits, and unto wizards that peep, and that mutter: should not a people seek unto their God? for the living to the dead? (Isa. 8:19 KJV)

But there was a man named Simon, who had previously practiced magic in the city and amazed the people of Samaria, saying that he himself was somebody great. They all paid attention to him, from the least to the greatest, saying, "This man is the power of God that is called Great." And they paid attention to him because for a long time he had amazed them with his magic. But when they believed Philip as he preached good news about the kingdom of God and the name of Jesus Christ, they were baptized, both men and women. Even Simon himself believed, and after being baptized he continued with Philip. And seeing signs and great miracles performed, he was amazed. (Acts 8:9–13 ESV)

As we were going to the place of prayer, we were met by a slave girl who had a spirit of divination and brought her owners much gain by fortune-telling. She followed Paul and us, crying out, "These men are servants of the Most High God, who proclaim to you the way of salvation." And this she kept doing for many days. Paul, having become greatly annoyed, turned and said to the spirit, "I command you in the name of Jesus Christ to come out of her." And it came out that very hour. (Acts 16:16–18 ESV)

Now Samuel was dead, and all Israel had mourned for him and buried him in his own town of Ramah. Saul had expelled the mediums and spiritists from the land. The Philistines assembled and came and set up camp at Shunem, while Saul gathered all Israel and set up camp at Gilboa. When Saul saw the Philistine army, he was afraid; terror filled his heart. He inquired of the Lord, but the Lord did not answer him by dreams or Urim or prophets. Saul then said to his attendants, "Find me a woman who is a medium, so I may go and inquire of her. "There is one in Endor," they said. So Saul disguised himself, putting on other clothes, and at night he and two men went to the woman. "Consult a spirit for me," he said, "and bring up for me the one I name." But the woman said to him, "Surely you know what Saul has done. He has cut off the mediums and spiritists from the land. Why have you set a trap for my life to bring about my death?" Saul swore to her by the Lord, "As surely as the Lord lives, you will not be punished for this." Then the woman asked, "Whom shall I bring up for you?" "Bring up Samuel," he said.

> When the woman saw Samuel, she cried out at the top of her voice and said to Saul, "Why have you deceived me? You are Saul!" The king said to her, "Don't be afraid. What do you see?" The woman said, "I see a ghostly figure coming up out of the earth." "What does he look like?" he asked. "An old man wearing a robe is coming up," she said. Then Saul knew it was Samuel, and he bowed down and prostrated himself with his face to the ground. Samuel said to Saul, "Why have you disturbed me by bringing me up?" "I am in great distress," Saul said. "The Philistines are fighting against me, and God has departed from me. He no longer answers me, either by prophets or by dreams. So I have called on you to tell me what to do." Samuel said, "Why do you consult me, now that the LORD has departed from you and become your enemy? The LORD has done what he predicted through me. The LORD has torn the kingdom out of your hands and given it to one of your neighbors—to David. Because you did not obey the LORD or carry out his fierce wrath against the Amalekites, the LORD has done this to you today. The LORD will deliver both Israel and you into the hands of the Philistines, and tomorrow you and your sons will be with me. The LORD will also give the army of Israel into the hands of the Philistines." Immediately Saul fell full length on the ground, filled with fear because of Samuel's words. His strength was gone, for he had eaten nothing all that day and all that night. (1 Samuel 28:3–20 NIV)

As we read the Word of God, we see that Jesus was confronted with people controlled by demon spirits on several occasions. These spirits always recognized the authority of Jesus. One of these examples occurred in Capernaum,

> There was in their synagogue a man with an unclean spirit. And he cried out, "What have you to do with us, Jesus of Nazareth? Have you come to destroy us? I know who you are—the Holy One of God." But Jesus rebuked him, saying, "Be silent, and come out of him!" And the unclean spirit, convulsing him and crying out with a loud voice, came out of him. (Mark 1:23–26 ESV)

Do Supernatural Hot Spots Exist?

I wanted to take this opportunity to talk about some of my personal supernatural experiences that occurred when I was a young boy and continued into my adulthood since we just confirmed what God's Word says about what we call the supernatural and or paranormal. The real-life events and experiences I am revealing here all occurred before the modern-day horror movies or books such as *The Birds*, Alfred Hitchcock's horror-thriller, and everything placed on the big screen after it.

Some examples of those productions yet to be born after our experiences were *Friday the 13th*, *Nightmare on Elm Street*, *Poltergeist*, *Night of The Living Dead*, *Child's Play*, *Amityville Horror*, *Pet Sematary*, *Salem's Lot*, to name a few. These occurrences started when my mother remarried about six years after our father had abandoned us. The man she married had an old two-story blockhouse that had no running water or electricity. Since there was no running water, the house had no plumbing in it other than a drain that ran to the outside from a sink that was sitting on top of a wooden frame in the kitchen. If you had to use the bathroom you went to the outhouse.

It was located in the country, and I was finally free of living in government projects and having to fight practically every day of my life even as a kid who was only in the first grade of elementary school. Three of my siblings had married by that time, so that left me and another brother Ronnie and sister Patty moving into this country environment where the poorest of the poor lived. Ronnie lived there only a year or less before he also got married and moved out of the house. That left me and my sister Patty, who was five years older than me.

We were not the first people to live there. From what I understand, that house was built in the midtwenties. Odd things did not occur right away. We did tell our mother that the noises at night were strange, but she said that was just the sounds of the house settling because it was old and that we would get used to it with time. My stepfather turned out to be a closet alcoholic who with time was drinking a fifth of whiskey a day. So he stayed in a drunken stupor most of the time and his hearing was bad due to his combat duty during World War II. We had two old Large bullseye oil lamps that were used for light during the night that mainly lit up the kitchen and the living room. My mother would escort Patty and me to the second floor where our bedrooms were with a candle since the lamps were made of glass and, when full of kerosene, were very heavy. Besides, we were climbing up thirteen steps to the second floor, and there was no handrail. After the light of the candle was gone, the rooms become extremely dark. There were no streetlights in the countryside of that part of Southwest Virginia. About a year passed and my mother and stepfather had saved enough money to get electricity put in the house and then the plumbing. I can still remember how happy my sister and I were. However, no bathroom with a commode was installed. It was discovered that the property was sitting on what had been some kind of site for dumping anything and everything. Even buried cars were found when they begin to dig for a septic tank. The outhouse remained the only source of a restroom until I left home.

Encounters and Strange Occurrences

After being in the house for a couple of years, the strange noises changed, and things began to happen that no one could explain. Patty and I had gone outside to escape the muggy heat that had been trapped inside the house during this particularly hot and sunny summer June day. Twilight's last glimmer of light was being chased away by stars, and the night sky was being unveiled for peering eyes and the creatures of the night. The estimated time we went to the porch was 8:30 p.m. We had a couple of the cheap folding aluminum chairs on the porch that we chose to sit in since the other old wicker chairs on the porch were aged and the reeds would pinch your legs and arms. The crickets were singing loud that night, and they were still laying their eggs. The strong smell of honeysuckle blooms was thick in the humid air that covered the far side of the Beaver Creek at the back of our house. My sister and I were talking about the star constellations, especially the big and little dipper. Our porch was facing a northeast direction.

Suddenly, it was like someone turned off the crickets, and the night became ominously quiet. Patty and I just looked at the sky, and there it was. An object moving probably three hundred feet above us. The object was as big as our house. It was in the shape of a disk with an intense lime green color and an outer white light around it. It made no noise other than what we both agreed was a pulsating humming noise with no exhaust. It was moving from west to east at a speed of what I would place at about twenty miles per hour. I tried to move and get up and run into the house, but I could not move. My eyes were transfixed on this craft as it moved over the peak of the treetops in the woods above our house.

The moment it disappeared, Patty and I both were able to move again, but we didn't run. We begin to argue about this thing that we mutually agreed was a UFO. I said it had gone to the top of the forest and landed, and Patty said it had just disappeared into the horizon. We were still talking and my sister said, "Brother, what is that?" As I looked to my left, this figure that was kind of human-looking was not walking but floating down the middle of our road toward our house. It had the same intense lime green color about it that the UFO had. We both got the same feeling of being paralyzed and could not talk, nor move. As this thing was almost directly in front of our house, it moved its head in a mechanical movement and looked straight at us. From the middle of the road to our front porch was no more than thirty feet away. It lingered for only a few seconds and went past our house into a sharp right curb. Still, clearly in our view, we watched it just disappear as it broke up into blobs of this green matter, which diminished into nothing, and it was gone.

As soon as that happened, my sister and I tore off of that porch so fast the chairs went flying. When we ran back into the house, my mom and stepfather had fallen asleep on the bed, but our mom sit straight up and said, "What in the name of God is going on, and why are you outside this time of night?" We tried to tell her what we had witnessed, but she said, "You're probably both so sleepy you are seeing things so go to bed now!"

When Patty and I looked at the clock on the wall, it was eleven thirty. My sister and I looked at each other in disbelief at the kitchen clock. We both agreed that it felt like we were on the porch for perhaps thirty minutes. We could not account for two and a half hours. In the following weeks after this sighting, some odd things happened to me and my sister. When in physical training in school, the boys were always trying to outdo one another. Someone starting a game that was take off running and try to run up the block wall until you had to jump down. When it was my turn, I could run up six to eight feet up the wall, and then I wouldn't jump down. I would run back down until the last foot and jump off of the wall. The guys were amazed since the best they could do was two to three feet. The coach came onto the floor, and they told him what I had done when asked to repeat it three times. I knew I couldn't let a grownup see this feat, so I just told them something like my head had started hurting. Big cherry-sized bumps would come on my arms and the amazing thing was that they would just vanish as quickly as they came.

Later, some men in suits came to my school, and I remember them taking me into a dark closet and scanning my body. They also took blood from me. After about three sessions of this, I finally asked my mother why this was happening. She went through the roof and came to my school and asked who permitted them to do anything to her son. They responded that it was health officials from Washington County that were doing the tests. My mom demanded to stop and then she said I need to know what they find immediately. My mom got a call a couple of days later from someone who said they were with the health department. They said they determined I had "blackbird disease" and then hung up. Those men in the suits never showed up again at my school. I was never given any medicine, and in a couple of weeks, the bumps ceased to appear.

My sister Patty's symptoms were different. She suddenly begins to bleed profusely as though she was on a constant menstrual cycle. The severe cramps would bend her double. My sister was rushed to the hospital three or four times, and the doctors were clueless as to why this just started occurring. After three weeks, the severe bleeding and the cramps just stopped without future occurrences.

The Uninvited

Occurrences of the unexplainable with supernatural and paranormal overtones begin to happen. Some of these events were repeated over and over. One night, my mom and stepfather were going out with another couple. It was on a weekend, and we were told that they may be late coming home. We were instructed if they weren't home by 10:00 p.m. to lock the front and back doors and get in bed. We had recently gotten a phone installed, which was in my mother's and stepfather's bedroom. My stepfather was so mean he had put a deadbolt on their bedroom door so we couldn't use the phone. I remember Patty and me trying to pick that lock to gain access to get on the phone. I had a sweetheart and Patty had a boyfriend, and we had their phone numbers. When either one of them would try to call our house, if my stepfather answered, he would tell them they had the wrong number or that we were not home.

During that time, no phone calls were received or made after 8:00 p.m. That was the rule of all households during this time. We did finally have electricity, and we had an old console black-and-white television set so we made an evening of it watching whatever we wanted on the three channels we could receive. The time passed quickly, and before you knew it, 10:00 p.m. was upon us and our mom and stepfather weren't home. We locked the front and back door, and we turned off the television. Patty and I hoped at least another fifteen minutes would pass so the television would cool down. My stepfather would feel the television to see if it was warm, and if it was, he would raise the roof on the house asking us why we were so late going to bed.

As Patty and I walked up the slick thirteen wooden steps, I had a habit of counting them. The last step made a horrible creaking sound when you stepped on it. All of the lights were off and the windows were open due to the smothering heat since it was in late August, and we didn't have a fan in the house. The road that we lived on didn't see much traffic at night, and when the little country store in sight of our house cut their lights off, the whole valley was pitch-black. There were rock cliffs that edged the road going from east to west. Most of the time, that is the direction our stepfather would come and go. You could hear our stepfather's old flathead six-cylinder Dodge station wagon most of the time before you could ever see it.

As any car entered our gravel driveway, it would echo on the walls of the house. Patty and I talked back and forth for a few minutes. Her bedroom was straight ahead as you topped the landing at the top of the steps, and my bedroom was to the immediate right. When we would become quiet, especially when nobody was home one would ask the other, "Are you awake?" This particular night, I laid there on my right side, looking out at the stars. Suddenly I heard a car enter the driveway. I remember thinking that was odd since the car must have come in the opposite direction that he normally would. I listened intensely as a car door slammed. Only one car door shut. I was then waiting for my mom and stepfather to come in to talk. Our mother would always come up and check on us.

Most of the time, she wouldn't say anything to either one of us. She would just stick her head in the door, observe us, and go back down the steps. I became concerned, but I didn't call out to my sister at that moment. Then there was a slow set of footsteps coming up the stairs. The type of footsteps that tell you that someone is sneaking deliberately, trying to go undetected. Thoughts were going through my mind at a hyperwarp speed. Like, why only one car door closed? Why don't I hear the usual conversation and footsteps of my mom and stepfather as they entered the house? The footsteps kept coming up the steps ever so slowly. My heart was pounding like a rabbit on the run. I sat up in my bed. I got on my knees and was crawling down to the bottom of my bed where the light switch to the overhead light was just within reach. Then I heard it whoever was on the steps placed their foot on that creaking top step and then eased back off of it again.

"Momma," my sister's voice pierced the silence, and my hair stood straight up as I lunged at the light switch. I was successful in turning the light switch to the on position, but I was pumping so much adrenaline I fell off the bottom of the bed just as the light I had just turned on popped and exploded. That fall hurt me badly, but I jumped up and ran into my sister's room where she was screaming at the top of her voice and in desperation turned on her ceiling light, simultaneously looking toward the steps. I shouted at my sister as my eyes fell upon an invisible intruder. There was nothing there. There was a light at the top of the steps, and I also turned on that light, feeling the air in front of me as to somehow touch with my hand what I could not see with my hands. My sister and I talked about what had just occurred. She had heard the car suddenly enter the driveway, one door shut, and nothing else until the footsteps begin on the staircase. We consoled each other, and then she helped me clean up the broken light bulb glass from the floor. Patty turned to me and said, "Little brother, this place is haunted."

The next noises we heard were the usual noises of our mother and stepfather coming home. I fell off to sleep in a sweat, not knowing what caused so much sweat. The heat or the fear.

Mirror Apparition

In my room, there was an antique tri-mirror window that was attached to a small one-drawer vanity. The drawer at that time was used to put both my underwear and socks in. One extremely hot summer night, I could get no relief from the heat and humidity. You know the kind of heat that makes you keep turning over your pillow to get to the cool side. I recall it was a starless night and overcast. I suddenly caught a movement out of the corner of my right eye. I turned my head and in the larger center mirror pane, I saw this ghostly figure. Just a white blur at first that started small and became bigger. Then I could see this was a woman dressed as though she was a Southern Belle complete with a chin strap to hold her bonnet on. She was running out of the distance in the mirror and it appeared as though there was a strong wind blowing about her. Her eyes were hollow, and for every second I looked at her, she appeared to be getting closer as though she would jump out of the mirror into my room. Again, my heart was racing with fear, and I quickly turned to my side, so I was facing away from the mirror. I didn't want to look back at the mirror. I knew I had to get to the light switch. I didn't crawl slowly this time. I sprang again, keeping low, and I hit the light switch. The ghostly figure in the mirror had vanished when I turned around. I couldn't believe my eyes. With the light still on, I walked over to my double windows to look out to see if perhaps the moon had come out and was shining into the room somehow causing this illusion. My eyes simply looked into a sky void of any light. I went back and cut the light off while standing at the bottom of my bed. I stood there for ten minutes or so and nothing showed up in the mirror. So I went back to my bed and went to sleep with my back toward the mirror. The same thing was repeated the following night. I took the same desperate measures to deal with this apparition with the same results.

I told my mom about it after the second occurrence. She came up into my room later and had a large Bible. She opened the Bible up about halfway and sat it on the dresser. I could hear her whisper a prayer and then she looked at me and said, "Son, don't ever close or move this Bible, do you understand?" I nodded my head yes, and she kissed me on the cheek and hugged me. The running woman never returned.

Night Moves and Noises

My sister and I both experienced something that to anyone I think would be terrifying. At first, I thought I was imagining things. I keep getting this sensation that something was under my bed. Like someone was lying on their back and pushing up into the mattress (no box springs on these beds) raising me. It happened to my sister first.

One night, she yelled out, "Mark, I'm going to tell mother that you are trying to scare me." I answered back from my room, and she immediately darted into my room. She was hysterical. She said something was pushing up on the small of her back under her bed and raising her in the air. This happened to both of us on several occasions. Our mother put flour under the beds, hoping that something would make some kind of impression; however, no impressions were ever made.

Another thing that would happen would be that something would slowly pull the sheets and blankets off of us. Most of the time, it was a slow movement, but I had the covers jerked completely off of me in one quick motion by an unseen hand. Heavy ashtrays would move across the table by themselves in the presence of both my sister and me. Doorknobs would be seen moving left and then right at our front door. We would turn on the porchlight, and nobody was there. We would lay at night and hear strange noises coming from the woods across the street from our house. Many times, we heard what sounded like a crying baby or a woman screaming. We had several cats so we knew the difference between cats fighting sounds and the sounds we heard. We would even hear an organ playing melodies out of the darkness of that forest that sounded like a funeral march. My sister and I finally concluded that these "things" were evil and they were taunting us.

These are but a few of the things that happened to me and my sister. I thought when I left that house that these things would stop, but they didn't. As an adult man, I would still hear whispers in rooms and see shadows moving across the floor. These occurrences were observed by other people at the same time. I started a commercial cleaning business, and odd things started happening at those buildings that had never occurred before. Car horns in parked cars would blow like someone was inside. This also happened to me at my own house, and to stop it, I had to disconnect the battery. Are there supernatural and paranormal hot spots? My answer, based upon my experiences, is yes.

CHAPTER 6

Where Did Evil Come From?

God created evil because he created all things. "I form the light, and create darkness: I make peace, and create evil: I the LORD do all these things" (Isa. 45:7 KJV).

This is also revealed in other scriptures. We know by his word that the good times and the bad times are created by him. "When times are good, be happy; but when times are bad, consider this: God has made the one as well as the other. Therefore, no one can discover anything about their future" (Eccles. 7:14 NIV). Jeremiah also declares, "Who has spoken and it came to pass, unless the Lord has commanded it? Is it not from the mouth of the Most High that good and bad come?" (Lam. 3:37–38 ESV). The scriptures themselves do not attribute moral wickedness to God, rather the scriptures proclaim just the opposite. "And Jesus said unto him, Why callest thou me good? there is none good but one, that is, God" (Mark 10:18 KJV). "The works of his hands are faithful and just; all his precepts are trustworthy" (Ps. 111:7 NIV). John proclaims, "This is the message we have heard from him and proclaim to you, that God is light, and in him is no darkness at all" (1 John 1:5). If God creates calamity, it has a righteous purpose. I think we can get a better understanding of this by looking at Adam and Eve.

Genesis 3:22 notes, "The man has now become like one of us, knowing good and evil. He must not be allowed to reach out his hand and take also from the tree of life and eat, and live forever."

God is speaking in this verse. The question arises: How exactly did knowing good and evil make man like God?

Adam and Eve already knew, intellectually, the difference between good and evil because of God's command to not eat of the tree's fruit. They knew it was right to eat of *those* trees and wrong to eat of *that* tree. However, when they chose to disobey, they knew evil *experientially* because they had sinned against God. At that point, they fully understood both right and wrong. God, who knows everything, already understood the nature of evil. When Adam and Eve lost their innocence, they, too, understood the nature of evil because of its very real presence within them. They became "like God" in that they now realized what evil was truly like.

The serpent's deception in the garden had included a grain of truth. Satan told Eve, "God knows that when you eat from it your eyes will be opened, and you will be like God, knowing good and evil" (Gen. 3:5). What the serpent did *not* say was that knowing evil would damage Adam and Eve's relationship with God. Half-truths can be as deceptive as lies. We know that Satan is the father of lies and liars. "Ye are of your father the devil, and the lusts of your father ye will do. He was a murderer from the beginning, and abode not in the truth, because there is no truth in him. When he speaketh a lie, he speaketh of his own: for he is a liar, and the father of it" (John 8:44 KJV).

It was enough for humans to understand and experience the good, and much good had been given to them (Gen. 1:31). But Adam and Eve wanted more knowledge and more experience, to their own detriment. The entry of sin into the world was a curse leading to a loss of fellowship with God and other judgments upon Adam and Eve. Those judgments have affected all humanity (Gen. 3:16–19). Only in the end, when God creates new heavens and a new earth, will this curse be broken. Revelation 21:3–4 promises,

> Look! God's dwelling place is now among
> the people, and he will dwell with them. They
> will be his people, and God himself will be with
> them and be their God. "He will wipe every tear

from their eyes. There will be no more death or mourning or crying or pain, for the old order of things has passed away."

Revelation 22:3 adds, "No longer will there be any curse."

Knowing good and evil was not a positive thing for Adam and Eve; rather, it served as the entry of sin into humanity. Now, all people sin and fall short of the glory of God (Rom. 3:23), and we all live under the twin curse of sin and death (Rom. 6:23). "Who will rescue me from this body that is subject to death? Thanks be to God, who delivers me through Jesus Christ our Lord!" (Rom. 7:24–25).

Can Our Deceased Loved Watch over Us?

Many times I have heard Hebrews used as the confirmation that their loved ones are in heaven and are watching over them. However, let us look at that particular scripture and see what is being referenced. "Therefore, since we are surrounded by so great a cloud of witnesses, let us also lay aside every weight, and sin which clings so closely, and let us run with endurance the race that is set before us" (Heb. 12:1 ESV).

The "great cloud of witnesses" is referring to the saints in chapter 11. They testify to God's faithfulness and the fact that he will see them through. Believing Jews living during the awful events during this time of tribulation. He was faithful in delivering them (Heb. 11:33–38). The race of Hebrews 12:1 by following the examples of the saints of old or that "great cloud of witnesses" of God's faithfulness and the importance of relying on him. So the answer is no, this is not our loved ones in "heaven." The author of the book of Hebrews is very debated. Some say it was written by Paul and others even say it was Moses. I can only say that it appears to have been written for Jewish Christians that lived in Jerusalem that were facing severe and horrific torture and tribulation. Its purpose was to lift or exhort those Christians facing these persecutions. Some scholars believe that the book of Hebrews was written for Jewish Christians who lived in

Jerusalem. Its purpose was to exhort Christians to persevere in the face of persecution.

Where Did Cain Find a Wife?

"Cain knew his wife, and she conceived and bore Enoch. When he built a city, he called the name of the city after the name of his son, Enoch" (Gen. 4:17).

An age-old question and one that agnostics and hecklers are fond of hurling at defenders of the authority of the Bible is, "Where did Cain get his wife?" To many who are not enemies of the Faith, such a question may cause unnecessary anxiety. As Adam and Eve were the first human pair on earth, and by natural generation had three sons who are named—Cain, Abel, Seth, and there is no mention of any named daughters it does seem as if there is a problem in knowing where the female came from whom Cain made his wife. In the genealogy of Adam, as the natural head of humanity, we are told that "Adam begat sons and daughters" (Gen. 5:4). How many sons there were, apart from the three named ones, and how many daughters were born to Eve we are not told. Because they lived long before the Sinaitic Laws were given, there was no moral difficulty involved in the marriage of near relatives. A good example of this is that Abraham married his half-sister Sarah. With Cain, the course was a necessary one as it was with his brothers they married their sisters. As we have already seen, Abraham married his half-sister, Sarah.

After the birth of Seth, Adam lived for another eight hundred years and died at the age of 930. When Eve died, we are not told, but if she lived as long as her husband, and she was able to continue procreation through the centuries, then the family of earth's first pair must have been large indeed. The register of births and deaths in Genesis 5 is an instructive record of remarkable longevity. The names of the earliest patriarchs are given, and the long years each of them lived upon the earth. If you add together the years that each one lived, you will find that their united lives cover a long period indeed. Enoch lived for the shortest period, 365 years—a year for every day of our normal year; while Methuselah lived the longest period of any known man, namely 969 years just thirty-one years short of a millennium. Adam lived for over one hundred years after the birth of Methuselah, and the latter would have been over three hundred years old when his grandson, Noah, was born. There is little room for doubt that Enoch, the seventh from Adam, had the privilege of conversing with earth's first man. By the end of the first two millenniums, the population of the earth through direct intermarriage must have been enormous.

As there may have been a lapse of many, many years before Cain's marriage, during such a period 130 years between the birth of Cain and Seth, the substitute for slain Abel—some of the unnamed sons and daughters of Adam and Eve were likely born. As there were no other humans on earth apart from their descendants, Cain, attracted to one of his sisters, took her to be his wife. Whomever the sister was who chose to go into banishment with her branded brother deserves credit for her willingness to share Cain's curse and wanderings. It is significant that they called their first child Enoch, which means "dedicated" and may suggest a change in Cain's character. The word is akin to "train" as found in the phrase, "Train up a child" (Prov. 22:6), and is also used in the dedication of a new house (Deut. 20:5). Cain called the city he built after the name of his son "Enoch" or "dedicated."

Nameless Women of the Bible

Noah's Wife and the Wives of His Son's

His father was Lamech and his mother is not named in the biblical accounts.

> And Noah was five hundred years old: and Noah begat Shem, Ham, and Japheth. (Gen. 5:32 KJV)

> And Noah was six hundred years old when the flood of waters was upon the earth. (Gen. 7:6 KJV)

> On that very day Noah and his sons, Shem, Ham, and Japheth, together with his wife and the wives of his three sons, entered the ark. (Gen. 7:13 ESV)

Noah's wife nor the wives of his sons are named. Noah had had a long life walking with God. During all those years in building the ark and finally loading the cargo of animals God told him to take, Noah's wife had to be a source of inspiration. The same could be said of the wives of Noah's sons. All the nations of the earth sprang from the children of the nameless wives of Shem, Ham, and Japheth, who bore their children after they settled again upon the earth. Noah was 950 years old when he died.

Shem's Daughters

While the genealogies of Ham and Japheth have some references to sons born to them, and to their successors, we have no mention of daughters although there must have been many of them. In Genesis 11:10–32, we know Shem had successors: Salah, Eber, Peleg, Reu, Serug, and Nahor. We have the repeated phrase "begat sons and *daughters.*" When Shem was one hundred years of age or about two years after the flood, he had or begat his firstborn, Arphaxad, and then lived for another five hundred years. In this time, we can be sure that he had numerous offspring. To replenish the earth, it was necessary, as at the beginning with Adam and Eve, for brothers to marry sisters. Thus, the children and grandchildren of Shem, Ham, and Japheth intermarried, and laid the foundation of the nations divided on the earth after the Flood.

Daughters of Men

And it came to pass when men began to multiply on the face of the earth, and daughters were born unto them, That the sons of God saw the daughters of men that they were fair; and they took them wives of all which they chose. And the LORD said, My spirit shall not always strive with man, for that he also is flesh: yet his days shall be a hundred and twenty years. There were giants in the earth in those days; and also after that, when the sons of God came in unto the daughters of men, and they bare children to them, the same became mighty men which were of old, men of renown. And God saw that the wickedness of man was great in the earth and that every imagination of the thoughts of his heart was only evil continually. And it repented the LORD that he had made man on the earth, and it grieved him at his heart. And the LORD said, I will destroy man whom I have created from the face of the earth; both man, and beast, and the creeping thing, and the fowls of the air; for it repenteth me that I have made them. But Noah found grace in the eyes of the LORD. (Gen. 6:1–8 KJV)

This is a portion of Scripture that has been variously interpreted. Who were the anonymous daughters of men who were mentioned three times? They were the offspring of men who began to multiply on the face of the earth and include some of the daughters already considered. Some suggest that these "daughters" with their cultivated beauty and corrupt ways were Cainites. They were descendants of the Cain who was the founder of civil institutions and social life, and "the sons of God" were "Sethites," pious men of noble rank. But there is no Scriptural evidence that either Seth or his descendants were known for their moral goodness, apart from Enoch. In our Lord's human genealogy Adam is called the son of God. "the son of Enos, the son of Seth, the son of Adam, the son of God" (Luke 3:38 ESV). This Interpretation suggests that the pious descendants of Seth entered alliances with the women of the corrupt race of Cain.

These marriages between pious men and inferior women could not have produced the giants that the scriptures speak of. "There were giants in the earth in those days; and also after that, when the sons of God came in unto the daughters of men, and they bare children to them, the same became mighty men which were of old, men of renown" (Gen. 6:4 KJV).

Regarding the great flood that overtook the world of the ungodly, Peter speaks of the angels that sinned and were cast out of heaven.

> For if God did not spare angels when they sinned, but cast them into hell and committed them to chains of gloomy darkness to be kept until the judgment; if he did not spare the ancient world, but preserved Noah, a herald of righteousness, with seven others, when he brought a flood upon the world of the ungodly. (2 Pet. 2:4–5 ESV)

Jude refers to these angelic beings as follows.

> And the angels who did not stay within their own position of authority, but left their proper dwelling, he has kept in eternal chains under gloomy darkness until the judgment of the great day just as Sodom and Gomorrah and the surrounding cities, which likewise indulged in sexual immorality and pursued unnatural desire, serve as an example by undergoing a punishment of eternal fire." (Jude 1:6–7 ESV)

Therefore, unique creatures emerged as the result of an illicit union. This necessitated a flood to cleanse the earth.

Peter's Wife and Mother-in-law

Neither Peter's wife nor his mother-in-law's names are mentioned in the scriptures. Although the Roman Catholic Church claims Peter as its first pope, this is found to be false according to God's Word. Both Peter's wife and her mother were living with them and we see that Jesus came to aid and to heal Peter's mother-in-law in their Capernaum home. "And when Jesus was come into Peter's house, he saw his wife's mother laid, and sick of a fever. And he touched her hand, and the fever left her: and she arose, and ministered unto them" (Mark 8:14–15 KJV).

Pharaoh's Daughter

One of the most fascinating stories in the Old Testament is the story of Moses. In Exodus, we see a new Pharaoh of Egypt emerge. While the previous king treated the Jews with favor this new king suppressed them and placed them into slavery. When they only seemed to get stronger out of fear, they would rise against him he made another creed.

> Then the king of Egypt said to the Hebrew midwives, one of whom was named Shiphrah and the other Puah, "When you serve as midwife to the Hebrew women and see them on the birthstool, if it is a son, you shall kill him, but if it is a daughter, she shall live." But the midwives feared God and did not do as the king of Egypt commanded them, but let the male children live. So the king of Egypt called the midwives and said to them, Why have you done this, and let the male children live?" The midwives said to Pharaoh, Because the Hebrew women are not like the Egyptian women, for they are vigorous and give birth before the midwife comes to them. So God dealt well with the midwives. And the people multiplied and grew very strong. And because the midwives feared God, he gave them families. (Exod. 1:15–21 ESV)

Since male Hebrew babies were in danger, the scriptures tell us the story of Moses's mother. Keep in mind his mother lived in Egypt where all of the descendants of Israel were oppressed.

> Now a man of the tribe of Levi married a Levite woman, and she became pregnant and gave birth to a son. When she saw that he was a fine child, she hid him for three months. But

when she could hide him no longer, she got a papyrus basket for him and coated it with tar and pitch. Then she placed the child in it and put it among the reeds along the bank of the Nile. His sister stood at a distance to see what would happen to him. (Exodus 2:1–4 NIV)

In this narrative, the mother of Moses is not named, however, she later is identified in the book of Exodus. "Amram married his father's sister Jochebed, who bore him Aaron and Moses. Amram lived 137 years" (Exod. 6:20 NIV).

As the basket with baby Moses floats down the Nile his destination by God takes place.

Now the daughter of Pharaoh came down to bathe at the river, while her young women walked beside the river. She saw the basket among the reeds and sent her servant woman, and she took it. When she opened it, she saw the child, and behold, the baby was crying. She took pity on him and said, "This is one of the Hebrews' children." Then his sister said to Pharaoh's daughter, "Shall I go and call you a nurse from the Hebrew women to nurse the child for you?" And Pharaoh's daughter said to her, "Go." So the girl went and called the child's mother. And Pharaoh's daughter said to her, "Take this child away and nurse him for me, and I will give you your wages." So the woman took the child and nursed him. When the child grew older, she brought him to Pharaoh's daughter, and he became her son. She named him Moses, "Because," she said, "I drew him out of the water." (Exod. 2:5–10 ESV)

In Hebrew, Moses means "to draw out."

Pharaoh's daughter, although nameless, in the scriptures played a huge part in God's plans for the entire nation of Israel. The Bible preserves her anonymity even though she is directly responsible for the freedom of the Jewish people from slavery at the hands of the nation of Egypt. Even though she was a "heathen woman" and an idolater who worshiped Ra the Egyptian sun god, she was chosen by the only true and living God. This nameless pagan woman who had a tender heart for a helpless crying baby Hebrew male child would raise him as her own until he was forty years old. He would acquire immense knowledge from the Egyptian culture "And Moses was learned in all the wisdom of the Egyptians, and was mighty in words and in deeds" (Acts 7:22 KJV). We do not know if this adopted mother of Moses was alive when Moses returned to Egypt forty years after he fled for his life to Midian after killing an Egyptian for beating a Hebrew slave. We only know she was Jehovah God's instrument to save a baby from death who became Moses, the servant of God.

Job's Wife

The story of Job is one of the best-known stories in the Bible. Debated and studied the book of Job is a great story of misery and great loss that the most faithful man on the face of the earth would suffer. If you are familiar with the story of Job then you must remember what his wife said to him Then his wife said to him, "Do you still hold fast your integrity? Curse God and die" (Job 2:9 ESV). In the English dictionary, *integrity* is defined as "the quality of being honest and having strong moral principles; moral uprightness." How man has warped the meaning of things. We know that someone honest, and with what we consider good moral principles would never consider suicide as a way out. That is exactly what his wife suggested that Job do. However, I will not speak lowly of Job's wife. She has witnessed the death of their ten children and the loss of everything they owned. All through this, she stayed by his side. We do not know her name although Job's daughters are named. "And he called the name of the first, Jemima; and the name of the second, Kezia; and the name of the third, Kerenhappuch" (Job 42:14 KJV). Remember the conversation between God and Satan? God told Satan he could take everything Job owned except his life. This included his children, his wife, and every animal and every material thing he owned and so it was.

Lot's Wife and Daughters

In Genesis 19, we read the narrative of the destruction of Sodom and Gomorrah. Neither the name of Lot's wife nor his daughters are ever mentioned or revealed in the scriptures. However, the two nameless daughters would alter history.

> After the two angels came we read their exact instructions to Lot "When he hesitated, the men grasped his hand and the hands of his wife and of his two daughters and led them safely out of the city, for the LORD was merciful to them. As soon as they had brought them out, one of them said, "Flee for your lives! Don't look back, and don't stop anywhere in the plain! Flee to the mountains or you will be swept away!" (Gen. 19:16–17 NIV)

The scriptures go on to tell us Lot's wife did not heed the angels warning and was turned into a pillar of salt as she turned back around for a final glance.

The account of the destruction of The now wifeless Lot ends up escaping to a cave with his two daughters.

> Lot and his two daughters left Zoar and settled in the mountains, for he was afraid to stay in Zoar. He and his two daughters lived in a cave. One day the older daughter said to the younger, "Our father is old, and there is no man around

here to give us children—as is the custom all over the earth. Let's get our father to drink wine and then sleep with him and preserve our family line through our father. That night they got their father to drink wine, and the older daughter went in and slept with him. He was not aware of it when she lay down or when she got up. The next day the older daughter said to the younger, "Last night I slept with my father. Let's get him to drink wine again tonight, and you go in and sleep with him so we can preserve our family line through our father." So they got their father to drink wine that night also, and the younger daughter went in and slept with him. Again he was not aware of it when she lay down or when she got up. So both of Lot's daughters became pregnant by their father. The older daughter had a son, and she named him Moab; he is the father of the Moabites of today. The younger daughter also had a son, and she named him Ben-Ammi he is the father of the Ammonites of today. (Gen. 19:30–38 NIV)

There are so many lessons to be learned from this story in God's Word. The first was we need to do what we are instructed to do or face the consequences like Lot's wife. We also can see what the influence of drinking to excess can lead to. In this instance, Lot took the virginity of both of his daughters while in a drunken stupor. This is where I mentioned his daughter's scheming would lead to a change of history. As a result of this unholy sexual union, the nations of Moab and Ammon were born. These two male babies would themselves both father two nations that would become the arch enemies of Israel. Later God would forbid Jews from intermarrying with the nations of Moab and Ammon.

CHAPTER 8

How Old Were the Disciples of Jesus?

Although none of the ages of the disciples of Christ are specifically revealed in the Bible, we can make certain if not accurate calculations. Since Jesus was approximately thirty years of age when he begins his ministry, we can look to Jewish culture and find that students or disciples were generally younger than their teacher. So we can assume with a great deal of certainty they were all several years younger than him. The scriptures would support this conclusion since Jesus referred to them as children. "Little children, yet a little while I am with you. You will seek me, and just as I said to the Jews, so now I also say to you, 'Where I am going you cannot come" (John 13:33 ESV). The only disciple we know who had a wife was Peter. In the time of Jesus, a Jewish man could receive a wife after the age of eighteen. Since the tradition of education during that time indicates this was the tradition of the day. We could "assume" that all of Jesus's disciples other than Peter were all under the age of eighteen since historically they entered the workforce by their mid-teens. Many were apprenticed under their fathers and worked for the prosperity of the family. James and John were already apprenticing in their trades when approached by Jesus.

"When he had gone a little farther, he saw James son of Zebedee and his brother John in a boat, preparing their nets. Without delay he called them, and they left their father Zebedee in the boat with the hired men and followed him" (Mark 1:19–20 NIV).

We have good solid ground through a study of God's Word to determine that all the disciples were under twenty years old except for Peter. That conclusion is found in the city of Capernaum and it involves the "temple tax."

> When they came to Capernaum, the collectors of the two-drachma tax went up to Peter and said, "Does your teacher not pay the tax?" He said, "Yes." And when he came into the house, Jesus spoke to him first, saying, "What do you think, Simon? From whom do kings of the earth take toll or tax? From their sons or from others?" And when he said, "From others," Jesus said to him, "Then the sons are free. However, not to give offense to them, go to the sea and cast a hook and take the first fish that comes up, and when you open its mouth you will find a shekel. Take that and give it to them for me and for yourself." (Matt. 17:24–27 ESV)

The shekel was enough to pay the taxes for Jesus and Peter only, even though the other disciples were present. Men under twenty were not required to pay roman taxes, including the temple tax.

Was the Earth Created before the Angels?

The short answer is no. I have heard many teach that during one of the six days of creation, God created the angels. We know that the angels were with God in heaven before the world itself was ever created simply by referencing God's Word. We can see this very clearly in God's conversation with Job.

> Where wast thou when I laid the foundations of the earth? Declare, if thou hast understanding. Who hath laid the measures thereof, if thou knowest? Or who hath stretched the line

upon it? Whereupon are the foundations thereof fastened? Or who laid the cornerstone thereof; When the morning stars sang together, and all the sons of God shouted for joy? (Job 38:4–7 KJV)

These verses in Job tell us the simple truth which is "all the sons of God" or the angels of heaven shouted for joy when the foundations of the earth itself were created by God.

Some declare that the war in heaven occurred before there was a "man to till the earth." Is that true? What does the Bible teach on this subject? First of all, let us see what the result of that war was. The account is in the twelfth chapter of Revelation.

And there was war in heaven: Michael and his angels fought against the dragon; and the dragon fought and his angels, 8 And prevailed not; neither was their place found any more in heaven. And the great dragon was cast out, that old serpent, called the Devil, and Satan, which deceiveth the whole world: he was cast out into the earth, and his angels were cast out with him. (Rev. 12:7–9 KJV)

Satan and his followers lost that war and they were kicked out of heaven by God himself. This war could not possibly have happened before the creation of Adam as the scriptures make it apparent such as is the case of the following verses.

Now there was a day when the sons of God came to present themselves before the LORD, and Satan also came among them. The LORD said to Satan, "From where have you come?" Satan answered the LORD and said, "From going to and fro on the earth, and from walking up and down on it." And the LORD said to Satan, "Have you

> considered my servant Job, that there is none like
> him on the earth, a blameless and upright man,
> who fears God and turns away from evil?" (Job
> 1:6–8 ESV)

It is natural to question how Satan appeared in heaven after the fact he had been cast out of heaven. "And he said unto them, I beheld Satan as lightning fall from heaven" (Luke 10:18 KJV). However, the scriptures are silent concerning the how and the why when we refer to Satan reappearing in heaven. This is one of the most fascinating passages in the Bible because we are invited into a scene through the scriptures where God is having a conversation with Satan. Many teach this is the only place where the devil and God have inter-reaction in the scriptures but this isn't the case.

In a vision of Joshua the High Priest, we read the following scripture where God rebukes Satan, "Then he showed me Joshua the high priest standing before the angel of the Lord, and Satan standing at his right hand to accuse him. And the Lord said to Satan, 'The Lord rebuke you, O Satan! The Lord who has chosen Jerusalem rebuke you! Is not this a brand plucked from the fire?'" (Zech. 3:1–2 ESV).

We also discover that the angels have a mission that directly involves the children of God who are born-again believers and these "sons of God" report back to God concerning their missions. "Are not all angels ministering spirits sent to serve those who will inherit salvation?" (Heb. 1:14 NIV).

We know that God is in complete control even when it comes to Satan, himself. The Lord already knows what our adversary is going to do and say. God is steering the enemy in the direction he desires, knowing the outcome.

How Old Was Jesus When Joseph Died?

There is nothing in the scriptures very descriptive about Joseph the earthly father of Jesus although many have guessed between the ages of eighteen to twenty-five. However, there is a scripture that suggests that Joseph was alive when Jesus started his ministry at around the age of thirty. "And Jesus himself began to be about thirty years of age, being (as was supposed) the son of Joseph, which was the son of Heli" (Luke 3:23 KJV). This occurred right after his baptism by his cousin John the Baptist.

In the book of John, it is confirmed that Joseph is still alive during the ministry of Jesus. "At this, the Jews there began to grumble about him because he said, 'I am the bread that came down from heaven.' They said, 'Is this not Jesus, the son of Joseph, whose father and mother we know? How can he now say, 'I came down from heaven'?" (John 6:41–42).

As the Jews have confirmed in this verse "whose father and mother we know" and not that we have known in the past tense. Therefore we can say that Joseph was still alive and that his death was before Jesus was thirty-three years of age since he is not found at Calvary and the crucifixion of Jesus.

CHAPTER 9

Who Is the Angel of the Lord?

After seeing the phrase "the angel of the Lord" as I read the scriptures, I just assumed that the reference could be just one of the tens of thousands of angels that God created. All Christians know that all of the faithful angels that fought Satan and a third of the angels that supported Lucifer's attempt to take over heaven are angels of God. However, I noticed that the angel referred to as the angel of the Lord was speaking in the first person.

The biblical story of Hagar's encounter with the angel of the Lord also shows the angel of the Lord and God speaking as one and the same person.

> And Sarai said to Abram, "May the wrong done to me be on you! I gave my servant to your embrace, and when she saw that she had conceived, she looked on me with contempt. May the LORD judge between you and me!" But Abram said to Sarai, "Behold, your servant is in your power; do to her as you please." Then Sarai dealt harshly with her, and she fled from her. The angel of the LORD found her by a spring of water in the wilderness, the spring on the way to Shur. And he said, "Hagar, servant of Sarai, where have you come from and where are you going?" She said,

"I am fleeing from my mistress Sarai." The angel of the LORD said to her, "Return to your mistress and submit to her." The angel of the LORD also said to her, "I will surely multiply your offspring so that they cannot be numbered for multitude." And the angel of the LORD said to her, "Behold, you are pregnant and shall bear a son. You shall call his name Ishmael, because the LORD has listened to your affliction. He shall be a wild donkey of a man, his hand against everyone and everyone's hand against him and he shall dwell over against all his kinsmen." So she called the name of the LORD who spoke to her, "You are a God of seeing," for she said, "Truly here I have seen him who looks after me." Therefore the well was called Beer-lahai-roi it lies between Kadesh and Bered. And Hagar bore Abram a son, and Abram called the name of his son, whom Hagar bore, Ishmael. Abram was eighty-six years old when Hagar bore Ishmael to Abram. (Gen. 16:5–16 ESV)

The name that the angel of the Lord gave to Hargar's unborn son which was Ishmael means "God hears."

We see the angel of the Lord in another passage of scripture talking to the woman who would bear one of the judges of Israel.

There was a certain man of Zorah, of the tribe of the Danites, whose name was Manoah. And his wife was barren and had no children. And the angel of the LORD appeared to the woman and said to her, "Behold, you are barren and have not borne children, but you shall conceive and bear a son. Therefore be careful and drink no wine or strong drink, and eat nothing unclean, for behold, you shall conceive and bear a son. No razor shall come upon his head, for the child shall be a Nazirite to God from the womb, and he shall begin to save Israel from the hand of the Philistines." Then the woman came and told her husband, "A man of God came to me, and his appearance was like the appearance of the angel of God, very awesome. I did not ask him where he was from, and he did not tell me his name, but he said to me, 'Behold, you shall conceive and bear a son. So then drink no wine or strong drink, and eat nothing unclean, for the child shall be a Nazirite to God from the womb to the day of his death.'"

Then Manoah prayed to the LORD and said, "O Lord, please let the man of God whom you sent come again to us and teach us what we are to do with the child who will be born." And God listened to the voice of Manoah, and the angel of God came again to the woman as she sat in the field. But Manoah her husband was not with her. So the woman ran quickly and told her husband, "Behold, the man who came to me the other day has appeared to me." And Manoah arose and went after his wife and came to the man and said to him, "Are you the man who spoke to this woman?" And he said, "I am." And Manoah said, "Now when your words come true, what is to be the child's manner of life, and what is his mission?" And the angel of the LORD said to Manoah, "Of all that I said to the woman let her be careful. She may not eat of anything that comes from the vine, neither let her drink wine or strong drink, or eat any unclean thing. All that I commanded her let her observe."

Manoah said to the angel of the LORD, "Please let us detain you and prepare a young goat for you." And the angel of the LORD said to Manoah, "If you detain me, I will not eat of your food. But if you prepare a burnt offering, then offer it to the Lord." (For Manoah did not know that he was the angel of the Lord.) And Manoah said to the angel of the Lord, "What is your name, so that, when your words come true, we may honor you?" And the angel of the Lord said to him, "Why do you ask my name, seeing it is wonderful?" So Manoah took the young goat with the grain offering, and offered it on the rock to the Lord, to the one who works wonders, and Manoah and his wife were watching. And when the flame went up toward heaven from the altar, the angel of the Lord went up in the flame of the altar. Now Manoah and his wife were watching, and they fell on their faces to the ground.

The angel of the Lord appeared no more to Manoah and to his wife. Then Manoah knew that he was the angel of the Lord. And Manoah said to his wife, "We shall surely die, for we have seen God." But his wife said to him, "If the Lord had meant to kill us, he would not have accepted a burnt offering and a grain offering at our hands, or shown us all these things, or now announced to us such things as these." And the woman bore a son and called his name Samson. And the young man grew, and the Lord blessed him. (Judges 13:2–24 ESV)

We see the angel of the Lord doing the will of the father in several places.

And that night the angel of the Lord went out and struck down 185,000 in the camp of the Assyrians. And when people arose early in the morning, behold, these were all dead bodies. (2 Kings 19:35 ESV).

> And God sent the angel to Jerusalem to
> destroy it, but as he was about to destroy it, the
> LORD saw, and he relented from the calamity. And
> he said to the angel who was working destruc-
> tion, "It is enough; now stay your hand." And
> the angel of the LORD was standing by the thresh-
> ing floor of Ornan the Jebusite. And David lifted
> his eyes and saw the angel of the LORD stand-
> ing between earth and heaven, and in his hand a
> drawn sword stretched out over Jerusalem. Then
> David and the elders, clothed in sackcloth, fell
> upon their faces. And David said to God, "Was
> it not I who gave command to number the peo-
> ple? It is I who have sinned and done great evil.
> But these sheep, what have they done? Please
> let your hand, O LORD my God, be against me
> and against my father's house. But do not let *the
> plague* be on your people. (1 Chron. 21:15–17
> ESV)

Note that David called the drawn sword of the angel of the Lord
a plague; therefore, the mighty sword of God can mean many things.

Jesus made it clear to the Jews that grumbled about whom he
said he was exactly who and from where he came.

> "For my Father's will is that everyone who
> looks to the Son and believes in him shall have
> eternal life, and I will raise them up at the last
> day." At this the Jews there began to grumble
> about him because he said, "I am the bread that
> came down from heaven." They said, "Is this not
> Jesus, the son of Joseph, whose father and mother
> we know? How can he now say, 'I came down
> from heaven'?" Stop grumbling among your-
> selves," Jesus answered. "No one can come to me
> unless the Father who sent me draws them, and

I will raise them up at the last day. It is written in the Prophets: 'They will all be taught by God.' Everyone who has heard the Father and learned from him comes to me. No one has seen the Father except the one who is from God; only he has seen the Father." (John 6:40–46 NIV)

We see the angel of the Lord visit another Judge of Israel.

The angel of the LORD came and sat down under the oak in Ophrah that belonged to Joash the Abiezrite, where his son Gideon was threshing wheat in a winepress to keep it from the Midianites. When the angel of the LORD appeared to Gideon, he said, "The LORD is with you, mighty warrior." Pardon me, my lord," Gideon replied, "but if the LORD is with us, why has all this happened to us? Where are all his wonders that our ancestors told us about when they said, 'Did not the LORD bring us up out of Egypt?' But now the LORD has abandoned us and given us into the hand of Midian." The LORD turned to him and said, "Go in the strength you have and save Israel out of Midian's hand. Am I not sending you?" "Pardon me, my lord," Gideon replied, "but how can I save Israel? My clan is the weakest in Manasseh, and I am the least in my family." The LORD answered, "I will be with you, and you will strike down all the Midianites, leaving none alive." Gideon replied, "If now I have found favor in your eyes, give me a sign that it is really you talking to me. Please do not go away until I come back and bring my offering and set it before you." And the LORD said, "I will wait until you return." Gideon went inside, prepared a young goat, and from an ephah of flour

> he made bread without yeast. Putting the meat in a basket and its broth in a pot, he brought them out and offered them to him under the oak. The angel of God said to him, "Take the meat and the unleavened bread, place them on this rock, and pour out the broth." And Gideon did so. Then the angel of the LORD touched the meat and the unleavened bread with the tip of the staff that was in his hand. Fire flared from the rock, consuming the meat and the bread. And the angel of the LORD disappeared. When Gideon realized that it was the angel of the LORD, he exclaimed, "Alas, Sovereign LORD! I have seen the angel of the LORD face to face!"

Again we see the angel of the Lord speaking directly to Gideon as God telling him that he will smite the Midianites. There is more discovery here I want to bring out before going on. The first is a question which is where did the Midianites come from? Let us allow God's Word to tell us. Abraham took another wife, whose name was Keturah. She bore him Zimran, Jokshan, Medan, Midian, Ishbak, and Shuah. Abraham was therefore the father of the Midianite tribe since they were the descendants of his son Midian.

The Kenites are mentioned several times in the Old Testament. The father-in-law of Moses, Jethro, was a Kenite, and as priest-leader of the tribe, he led in the worship of Yahweh, whom Moses later revealed to the Hebrews as their own God whom they had forgotten. The Kenites were a tribe related to the Midianites and the Israelites.

So our collection of available information leads us to question if the Israelites were related to the Midianites why was Gideon going to war against them? The answer is that Israel once again turned away from God and worshiped other gods so God turned them over to the Midianites. Then they suffered when Midianites and their allies such as the Amalekites destroyed their crops and stole their livestock, reducing the Israelites to starvation. Israel was oppressed by the Midianites for seven years until Gideon was instructed by God to war against them.

In many cases, we are seeing the second part of the trinity manifesting itself. The angel of the Lord was speaking as though he was God himself. He was unique over all of the other angels. A good example of this is as follows. "But the angel of the LORD called to him from heaven and said, "Abraham, Abraham!" And he said, "Here I am" (Gen. 22:11 ESV) and in the next verse we find the confirmation. "Do not lay a hand on the boy," he said. "Do not do anything to him. Now I know that you *fear God*, because you have not withheld *from me* your son, your only son" (Gen. 22:12 ESV). This scripture equates the angel of the Lord and God as one.

The angel of the Lord is Jesus Christ, one of the Godhead three in the Holy Trinity. Jesus confirmed that he and God were one. "I and my Father are one" (John 10:30 KJV).

"Let not your hearts be troubled. Believe in God; believe also in me" (John 14:1 ESV).

> He is the image of the invisible God, the firstborn of all creation. For by him all things were created, in heaven and on earth, visible and invisible, whether thrones or dominions or rulers or authorities—all things were created through him and for him. And he is before all things, and in him all things hold together. And he is the head of the body, the church. He is the beginning, the firstborn from the dead, that in everything he might be preeminent. For in him all the fullness of God was pleased to dwell, and through him to reconcile to himself all things, whether on earth or in heaven, making peace by the blood of his cross. (Col. 1:15–20 ESV)

CHAPTER 10

The Story Inside of Jonah and the Whale: Is Everyone My Brothers and Sisters in Christ?

The Story Inside of Jonah and the Whale

There is a story deep in the belly of this story. If we dare to go below the surface of this story then perhaps, we will discover the "whale" is not the main focus in his amazing story. There is nothing in the scriptures that

There is a story deep in the belly of this story. If we dare to go below the surface. Before we dig further, we need to establish that the Bible does not refer to the fish as a whale at all.

"And the LORD appointed a great fish to swallow up Jonah. And Jonah was in the belly of the fish three days and three nights" (Jonah 1:17 ESV). I have heard several sermons on Jonah. I heard that the three days and nights were significant because it was the same amount of time that the body of our savior laid in the tomb after his crucifixion and I admit that time frame was significant and not just a coincidence. I have heard other sermons that state this is a good example of the consequences of rebellion toward God can result in. Another sermon I heard was focused on the supernatural powers of God that are used to rescue his people. I agree with all of the sermons, but now I have one of my own if you will allow this as part of our journey for the truth.

We all know that the entire book of Jonah is about a reluctant prophet who flees when God tells him to go to Nineveh to warn its people of the coming disaster because of that city's wickedness. Instead of going to Nineveh as God told him to do Jonah boards a ship to Tarshish instead of obeying God. Let us examine the account of Jonah.

Now the word of the LORD came to Jonah the son of Amittai, saying, "Arise, go to Nineveh, that great city, and call out against it, for their evil has come up before me." But Jonah rose to flee to Tarshish from the presence of the LORD. He went down to Joppa and found a ship going to Tarshish. So he paid the fare and went down into it, to go with them to Tarshish, away from the presence of the LORD.

But the LORD hurled a great wind upon the sea, and there was a mighty tempest on the sea, so that the ship threatened to break up. Then the mariners were afraid, and each cried out to his god. And they hurled the cargo that was in the ship into the sea to lighten it for them. But Jonah had gone down into the inner part of the ship and had lain down and was fast asleep. So the captain came and said to him, "What do you mean, you sleeper? Arise, call out to your god! Perhaps the god will give a thought to us, that we may not perish."

And they said to one another, "Come, let us cast lots, that we may know on whose account this evil has come upon us." So they cast lots, and the lot fell on Jonah. Then they said to him,

"Tell us on whose account this evil has come upon us. What is your occupation? And where do you come from? What is your country? And of what people are you?" And he said to them, "I am a Hebrew, and I fear the Lord, the God of heaven, who made the sea and the dry land." Then the men were exceedingly afraid and said to him, "What is this that you have done!" For the men knew that he was fleeing from the presence of the Lord, because he had told them.

Then they said to him, "What shall we do to you, that the sea may quiet down for us?" For the sea grew more and more tempestuous. He said to them, "Pick me up and hurl me into the sea; then the sea will quiet down for you, for I know it is because of me that this great tempest has come upon you." Nevertheless, the men rowed hard to get back to dry land, but they could not, for the sea grew more and more tempestuous against them. Therefore, they called out to the Lord, "O Lord, let us not perish for this man's life, and lay not on us innocent blood, for you, O Lord, have done as it pleased you." So, they picked up Jonah and hurled him into the sea, and the sea ceased from its raging. Then the men feared the Lord exceedingly, and they offered a sacrifice to the Lord and made vows. (Jonah 1:1–16 ESV)

The first chapter of Jonah is a revelation of many things. Jonah was very much like most of us. He had his unique good and bad qualities even as a prophet. We see in verse three that Jonah disobeys God and then attempts the impossible. He tries to flee from the presence of God. We then read in verse 4 that God evokes a great wind upon the sea so bad that the crew of the ship thought the ship will be ripped apart. In verse 5 we read where each of the mariners cried out to "his God," and they became so desperate they begin to throw cargo on the ship into the sea to lighten their load. What was Jonah doing during this time? He was asleep in the inner part of the ship, and when they do, the captain sees him asleep and is appalled and demands Jonah to call out to "his God" so that they may not perish. They then cast lots to determine who has brought "this evil upon us." The lot fell upon Jonah. Just for some that may not know the casting of lots is not just a random game of chance so to speak like rolling dice or drawing a card. It was believed that the casting of lots was to reveal the will of God. Let us keep in mind this is not some kind of unusual ritual rarely practiced.

In biblical times, it was practiced by Jews and Gentiles. It is a fact, that the Lord's disciples cast lots to see who would replace Judas who had hung himself after betraying Jesus. An account of this is found in Acts 1:21–26 and the lot fell upon Matthias who became the replacement for Judas and to bring the discipleship back to a total of twelve men. We also see in the book of John that Roman soldiers did it at the crucifixion of Jesus.

> When the soldiers crucified Jesus, they took his clothes, dividing them into four shares, one for each of them, with the undergarment remaining. This garment was seamless, woven in one piece from top to bottom. "Let's not tear it," they said to one another. "Let's decide by lot who will get it." This happened that the scripture might be fulfilled that said, "They divided my clothes among them and cast lots for my garment." (John 19:23–24 NIV)

The prophecy in question occurred one thousand years before Christ in Psalm 22:18 (NIV).

The mariners in verse 8 questioned Jonah about what evil he has done and what was his occupation is and his country. Jonah told them he was a Hebrew and tells them he worships the God of heaven who created everything. They then asked him what they should do to quiet the storm. It was then Jonah said, "Pick me up and hurl me into the sea; then the sea will quiet down for you, for I know it is because of me that his great tempest has come upon you" (Jonah 1:12 ESV). I must point out that the crew of this ship were decent men because despite what Jonah said they proceeded to row hard to get back to dry land but it was all in vain. Then in verses 14–16 the mariners prayed to God that they were doing the right thing as they hurled Jonah into the sea that then became ominously quiet. The men then were fearful of the Lord and offered a sacrifice to him and made vows. Then we read that God summons a great fish to swallow up Jonah where he prayed for three days to God before God made the fish vomit him upon dry land.

We can learn several things from Jonah. At the top of the list would be that we should never try to run from God nor refuse to do his will. I think, however, the most profound lesson here comes in the form of questions that apply to all of us. The first question would be "Who or what is your Jonah that you need to throw overboard or out of your life to quiet the storms in your life?" Many Jonah's come in many different assortments and disguises. I discovered after my self-examination that I had several! What were my Jonah's? Well, I had to throw pride and ego overboard right away. Then I threw envy and enmity overboard. Those are the ones that came to mind right after I had an honest discussion with my soul. You know that God resists the proud and ego will just flat out destroy your witness. Envy is something as simple as a thought such as "I wish I could be that lucky." Enmity just sounds bad, doesn't it? Well, this can be a case of becoming very angry after being cut off by another driver. Modern society calls it road rage. What do you need to throw overboard? Are you guilty of not telling the truth? How about not correcting the cashier when they give you back more money than you have coming to you? Do you fudge on your taxes? Do you handle trashy or lewd language? Do you tell distasteful jokes?

I got rid of a lot of Jonah's when I became a Christian, but some of them must have clung onto the side of the boat. Because from time to time I catch them crawling back in and after having a good long prayer with the Lord, I fling them overboard. Make up a list and be honest about it friends. It will surprise you how many Jonah's are stowed away on your ship on this journey we call life.

What Are the Seven Deadly Sins?

I remember when I was young hearing discussions about the seven deadly sins. My response then was why are seven particular sins so deadly? Then as an adult I thought according to the Bible was in Romans 6:23, "For the wages of sin *is* death, but the gift of God *is* eternal life in Christ Jesus our Lord." Therefore, all sin is deadly in a spiritual way."

I did search the Bible to see if these seven deadly sins were mentioned. I couldn't find them because they are not God's words. They are the words of theology. I found that these seven deadly sins or seven cardinal sins were part of Roman Catholic theology.

According to this theology, there are seven sins that further induce more immoral behavior. Pope Gregory I the Great in the sixth century enumerated them as follows: (1) vainglory or pride, (2) greed or covetousness, (3) lust or inordinate or illicit sexual desire, (4) envy, (5) gluttony which is usually included drunkenness, (6) wrath or anger, and (7) sloth, which is defined as a failure to do things that one should do, though the understanding of the sin in antiquity was that this laziness or lack of work was simply a symptom of the vice of apathy or indifference, particularly an apathy or boredom with God. All of these could be overcome by the virtues (corresponding numerically) of (1) humility, (2) charity, (3) chastity, (4) gratitude, (5) temperance, (6) patience, and (7) diligence.

Does the Bible Mention Dinosaurs?

Archeologists have made many physical discoveries that have proven dinosaurs once existed, but the Bible does not talk about dinosaurs in the way modern education would present them. The Bible does not catalog every creature God ever created. There are three creatures mentioned in the Bible that are monstrous in size and abilities.

> Behold, Behemoth, which I made as I made you; he eats grass like an ox. Behold, his strength in his loins, and his power in the muscles of his belly. He makes his tail stiff like a cedar; the sinews of his thighs are knit together. His bones are tubes of bronze, his limbs like bars of iron. He is the first of the works of God; let him who made him bring near his sword! (Job 40:15–19 ESV)

Notice the last verse states, "He is the first of the works of God."

This passage describes this creature in detail. Because of its colossal physical attributes, it is clearly something that is a monstrosity. The only thing we know that even comes close to this is a dinosaur. This one it would seem lives on dry land.

The second creature is revealed in the book of Psalm. "You divided the sea by your might; you broke the heads of the sea monsters on the waters. You crushed the heads of Leviathan; you gave him as food for the creatures of the wilderness" (Ps. 74:13–14 ESV).

The second creature is much greater than the Leviathan or sea serpents because the foregoing scripture plainly states he "divides the sea by his strength" and this creature crushes the heads of the Sea Serpents and according to the scriptures although he gets the serpents from the sea he leaves them on dry land for "the creatures of the wilderness."

The third creature is the Leviathan or the monster of the sea, which is plainly described in this scripture from Isaiah.

"In that day, the LORD will punish with his sword his fierce, great and powerful sword Leviathan the gliding serpent, Leviathan the coiling serpent; he will slay the monster of the sea" (Isa. 27:1 NIV).

Is Everyone My Brothers and Sisters in Christ?

I have heard many times Christians refer to all mankind as their brothers and sisters because in God's eyes we are all the same. Spiritually speaking from the Word of God nothing is further from the truth.

> And his mother and his brothers came and standing outside they sent to him and called him. And a crowd was sitting around him, and they said to him, "Your mother and your brothers are outside, seeking you." And he answered them, "Who are my mother and my brothers?" And looking about at those who sat around him, he said, "Here are my mother and my brothers! For whoever does the will of God, he is my brother and sister and mother. (Mark 3:31–35 ESV).

Jesus makes it clear that "whoever does the will of God" are our true brothers and sisters spiritually speaking.

CHAPTER 11

Myth Busters

Firstly, I am using the word *myth*, defined as "a widely held false belief or idea."

That applies to phrases that claim biblical origin that has been used in some cases for hundreds of years. Some things that people quote as the "gospel truth" are in some cases not biblical at all. This doesn't mean that their origins don't project pure intentions. On the other hand, many people use many phrases unaware that their root source is the Bible. Before we search out the truth can you find which ones are directly from the Word of God and which ones are not before going on? If you elect to say that it isn't in the Bible can you try and guess the origin of the phrase? Try it and then let us look at each one.

"God won't put more on you than you can stand."

"Suffer fools gladly."

"Let the blind lead the blind."

"The eyes are the windows to the soul."

"The lion will lay down with the lamb."

"God helps those who help themselves."

"A wolf in sheep's clothing."

"This too shall pass."

"Suffer fools gladly."

"Go the extra mile."

"The truth will set you free."

"Charity begins at home."

"By the skin of your teeth"

"Money is the root of all evil."

"Pride comes before the fall."

"Cleanliness is next to godliness."

"A fool and his money are soon parted."

"By his stripes, we are healed."

"Fight the good fight."

"God helps those that help themselves."

"God won't put more on you than you can stand."

This is another quotation not found in the scriptures. This phrase is often referring to pain and suffering or emotional distress. This phrase is derived from the following scripture: "There hath no temptation taken you but such as is common to man: but God is faithful, who will not suffer you to be tempted above that ye are able; but will with the temptation also make a way to escape, that ye may be able to bear it" (1 Cor. 10:13 KJV).

"Suffer fools gladly." This phrase tends to partially stem from the King James Version, which says, "For ye suffer fools gladly, seeing ye yourselves are wise" (2 Cor. 11:19 KJV). The English Standard Version reads, "For you gladly bear with fools, being wise yourselves!" The New International Version reads, "You gladly put up with fools since you are so wise!"

"Go the extra mile." When we say "go the extra mile" we mean to do more than you're obligated to do and go the extra mile. During the Roman occupation of the Holy Land during the time of Christ, this was a law of the land. Which stated that if you were asked by a Roman soldier to carry equipment for him, you had to do it for one mile. Jesus said to do more than what is required of you.

"Let the blind lead the blind." This is in part from the scriptures. "Let them alone: they be blind leaders of the blind. And if the blind lead the blind, both shall fall into the ditch" (Matt. 15:14 KJV).

"The eyes are the windows to the soul." Matthew 6:22 ESV says, "The eye is the lamp of the body. So, if your eye is healthy, your whole body will be full of light." As we can see there was no reference to the soul at all. Some attribute this quote originated by writers such as Shakespeare or Milton.

"The lion will lay down with the lamb." This is a direct misquote from Isaiah 11:6 (ESV) that says, "The wolf shall dwell with the lamb, and the leopard shall lie down with the young goat, and the calf and the lion and the fattened calf together; and a little child shall lead them." The only two animals here that God mentions as lying down together are the leopard and the young goat.

"God helps those who help themselves." I have personally heard my mother and many others make this statement decades ago. Research reveals that the phrase comes from an article called "Discourses Concerning Government" written by Algernon Sydney. Ben Franklin then uses the phrase in Poor Richards's Almanac in 1757, and it caught on as something that was straight from the scriptures.

"A wolf in sheep's clothing." This phrase is often used often to describe others and although this quote is not a direct quote from the Bible that is its true source. "Beware of false prophets, who come to you in sheep's clothing but inwardly are ravenous wolves" (Matt. 7:15 ESV).

"This, too, shall pass." Although this cannot be directly found in any versions of the Christian Bible it could be a misquote of Deuteronomy 28:15 (KJV), "But it shall come to pass, if thou wilt not hearken unto the voice of the LORD thy God, to observe to do all his commandments and his statutes which I command thee this day; that all these curses shall come upon thee, and overtake thee." The King James Version is the only version that comes close. "This phrase was found to have Muslim origins from a Persian Sufi in the Middle Ages.

"The truth will set you free." This is a partial quote from biblical scripture. "And you will know the truth, and the truth will set you free" (John 8:32 ESV).

"Charity begins at home." Again another widely misapplied phrase that doesn't come from the pages of the Bible. Where its original origins are subject to debate, however, we do know that Sir Thomas Browne wrote the phrase in 1642.

"By the skin of your teeth." This is also a partial quote from scripture that says, "My bone cleaveth to my skin and to my flesh, and I am escaped with the skin of my teeth" (Job 19:20 KJV).

"Money is the root of all evil." This scripture is misquoted all the time. First Timothy 6:10 (ESV) says, "For the love of money is the root of all evils." Money in and of itself isn't the problem. Rather the "root cause" is the love of it. Many people put money first in their lives before anything else. This includes many things. Another great example is football. Is it no coincidence that the rulers of football decided in 1967 to have the Super Bowl on Sunday afternoons, which tempted countless thousands of Christians out of Sunday evening church services. God has forbidden putting anything before him. "You shall have no other gods before me" (Exod. 20:3 ESV). It could be rightly said that the moral value of money is in the hands of the person that has possession of it. Money can be used for either good or bad things.

"Pride comes before the fall." Although this is a misquote its true origin is unknown. Proverbs 16:18 (ESV) says, "Pride goes before destruction, and a haughty spirit before a fall."

"Cleanliness is next to godliness." This phrase does not come from the scriptures although the Jews under Mosaic Law were very particular about cleanliness and purity and the book of Leviticus demonstrates that discipline the quote still wasn't inspired by divine guidance. We do know that John Wesley took a phrase from Frances Bacon and changed it into the phrase we see today.

"A fool and his money are soon parted." Even though a lot of people can relate to this phrase, it is not heaven-sent. It comes from *Five Hundred Pointes of Good Husbandrie* by Thomas Tusser back in 1573.

"By his stripes, we are healed." This phrase is extracted in part from the following scripture. "But he was wounded for our transgressions, he was bruised for our iniquities: the chastisement of our peace was upon him, and with his stripes, we are healed" (Isaiah 53:5 KJV). This phrase is used much of the time referring to how we will be physically healed when we become critically ill through the stripes that Jesus bore on Calvary. When looking at the entire passage we can see there is no reference to physical healing. The focus of this verse is entirely upon the spiritual healing we have received through the suffering of Christ Jesus.

"Fight the good fight." "Fight the good fight of the faith. Take hold of the eternal life to which you were called and about which you made the good confession in the presence of many witnesses" (1 Timothy 6:12 ESV). These words come from the Apostle Paul who wrote to Timothy from prison, encouraging him to fight for his faith. In our present society, we use it as a phrase to overcome obstacles.

"God helps those that help themselves." This is very popular phrase is not from the scriptures. The phrase "God helps those who help themselves" is a motto that emphasizes the importance of self-initiative and agency. The expression is known around the world and is used to inspire people to self-help. The phrase originated in ancient Greece as "the Gods help those who help themselves" and may originally have been proverbial. It is illustrated by two of Aesop's fables and a similar sentiment is found in ancient Greek drama. Although it has been commonly attributed to Benjamin Franklin, the modern English wording appears earlier in Algernon Sidney's work.

What Are the Details of the Crucifixion of Jesus Christ?

Crucifixion sometimes began with a scourging or flogging of the victim's back. This was the case of our savior. The Romans used a whip called a *flagrum*, which consisted of small pieces of bone and metal attached to many leather strands. The number of blows given to Jesus is not recorded; however, the number of blows in Jewish law was thirty-nine (one less than the forty called for in the Torah, to prevent a counting error). During the scourging, the skin was ripped from the back, exposing a bloody mass of tissue and bone. Extreme blood loss occurred. Many that were flogged like Jesus died before a crucifixion could take place. In addition to the flogging, Jesus faced severe beatings and torment by the Roman soldiers, which included the plucking of His beard and the piercing of his scalp with a crown of thorns. Every act of torture by the Romans spilled the blood of Christ.

After the flogging, the victim was often forced to carry his cross, or patibulum, to the execution site. The cross could easily weigh 100 pounds. In the case of Jesus, the record shows that Jesus carried his cross the distance of over two football fields. In a weak and tormented state, it's no wonder the record establishes that Jesus needed a great deal of assistance along this path to Calvary. Once the victim arrived at the execution site, the cross was put on the ground and the victim was forced to lie upon it. Spikes about seven inches long and three-eighths of an inch in diameter were driven into the wrists. The spikes would hit the area of the median nerve, causing shocks of pain up the arms to the shoulders and neck. Already standing at the crucifixion site would be the seven-foot-tall post, called a stipes. In the center of the stipes was a crude seat to "support" the victim. The cross was then lifted onto the stipes, and the victim's body was turned on the seat so that the feet could be nailed to the stipes. At this point, there was tremendous strain put on the wrists, arms, and shoulders, resulting in a dislocation of the shoulder and elbow joints. The position of the nailed body held the victim's rib cage in a fixed position, which made it extremely difficult to exhale, and impossible to take a full breath. Having suffered from the scourging, the beatings, and the walk with the cross. At this point, Jesus would have been extremely weak and dehydrated. He had lost significant amounts of blood. As time passed, the loss of blood and lack of oxygen would cause severe cramps, spasmodic contractions, fainting, and unconsciousness.

Ultimately, the mechanism of death in crucifixion was suffocation. To breathe, the victim was forced to push up on his feet to allow for inflation of the lungs. Taking into account that a normal man breathes in twelve to twenty breaths per minute every passing minute was agony. As the body weakened and pain in the feet and legs became unbearable, the victim was forced to exchange breathing for pain and exhaustion as blood and life were ebbing away. Eventually, the victim would succumb in this way, becoming utterly exhausted or lapsing into unconsciousness so that he could no longer lift his body off the stipes and inflate his lungs. Due to the shallow breathing, the victim's lungs would begin to collapse in areas, which would also cause a faster heart rate. Due to the loss of blood from the scourging, the victim probably experiencing tremors and spasms, resulting in an increased strain on the heart, which beats faster to compensate. Fluid would also build up in the lungs. Under the stress put on the heart, many victims would die of heart failure. There are several different theories and opinions about what exactly killed the son of God in the body of this man called Jesus. Regardless of the actual medical cause of final death, we can all agree on one thing. Jesus suffered six hours of horrible and sustained torture on the cross of Calvary. The crucifixion accounts of Jesus Christ are in entire agreement with the practices of the Romans in that period. When I try to comprehend that terrible event and the pain and suffering he endured, I have often wondered what thoughts were going through his mind in those six brutal hours. I wonder as he looked out at the crowd, did he see any people he had healed? Did he have flashbacks to the beginning when he was born and how he was loved and cherished on Christmas morn? One thing the scriptures do tell us is that in his last hours on this earth as a mere man he was concerned about others above all else. His first words from the cross were, "Then said Jesus, Father, forgive them; for they know not what they do. And they parted his raiment, and cast lots" (Luke 23:34 KJV). He thought of His mother, who stood by the cross weeping. "When Jesus saw his mother and the disciple whom he loved standing nearby, he said to his mother, "Woman, behold, your son!" Then he said to the disciple, "Behold, your mother!" And from that hour the disciple took her to his own home" (John 19:26–27 ESV). Jesus was able and had the authority to forgive sins as one of the two thieves made a request of him while the other one cursed him.

> One of the criminals who hung there hurled insults at him: "Aren't you the Messiah? Save yourself and us!" But the other criminal rebuked him. "Don't you fear God," he said, "since you are under the same sentence? We are punished justly, for we are getting what our deeds deserve. But this man has done nothing wrong." Then he said, "Jesus, remember me when you come into your kingdom. Jesus answered him, "Truly I tell you, today you will be with me in paradise." (Luke 23:39–43 NIV)

Finally, Jesus expressed his complete surrender to the will of God as He said, "It is finished" (John 19:30). "Father, into Thy hands I commend My spirit" (Luke 23:46). Investigate the historical record and then examine your heart. Jesus gave Himself willingly for you and me. Jesus suffered a horrible death for you and me. Jesus loved us so much that He willingly died in utter shame and pain for our sins. In fact, the Bible teaches us that He who was without sin was literally "made sin" for us. God, in human form, allowed himself to be made sin to save us. On the cross, he bore all the world's sin because of His love. The only way to complete His story of love is to love Him in return.

Who Were the Thieves on the Cross?

The scriptures do not give a lot of details on the two thieves on the cross that were crucified on either side of Jesus in the Gospel of Luke. However, Flavius Josephus (AD 37–c. 100), a Jewish historian born in Jerusalem four years after the crucifixion of Jesus of Nazareth, was in the same city. Because of this proximity to Jesus in terms of time and place, his writings have a near-eyewitness quality as they relate to the entire cultural background of the New Testament era. But their scope is much wider than this, encompassing also the world of the Old Testament. His two greatest works are *Jewish Antiquities*, unveiling Hebrew history from the Creation to the start of the great war with Rome in AD 66, while his *Jewish War*, though written first, carries the record on to the destruction of Jerusalem and the fall of Masada in AD.

In the Gospel of Luke, we are told that during Our Blessed Lord's crucifixion, two other men were suffering the same death, one to either side of Him. The one to Christ's right has become known as the "good thief" while the one to His left is referred to as the "unrepentant thief."

While the Gospels do not mention specific names, tradition tells us the good thief was named St. Dismas, and the unrepentant thief, Gestas.

While both men were suffering the same gruesome execution and were both in the presence of Christ, their reactions to their situation are quite different. Gestas reviles Our Lord and says, "Are You not the Messiah? Save Yourself and us" (Luke 23:39). Gestas asks to come down from his cross.

But Dismas does not ask to be taken down. Dismas rebukes Gestas and proclaims Christ's innocence, and in one of the most startling and beautiful moments of the Gospel, does not ask to be taken down from his sure and painful death. He asks, instead, to be taken up with Christ, saying "Jesus, remember me when You come into Your kingdom" (Luke 23:42). Jesus replies to St. Dismas, saying, "Amen, I say to you, today you will be with Me in Paradise."

This is the lesson of St. Dismas, who accepted his cross and placed his hope not in this world, but in the promise of the next. Which of these two are you? Do wish to come down from your cross and continue to be of this earth, or do you wish to accept your cross and be taken up to Christ in the life to come? Gestas was only twelve feet from salvation yet he didn't accept it. If you haven't surrendered your life to Jesus, I urge you to do it now. You are much closer to the Lord than the twelve feet that separated Gestas from Jesus. You are only one prayer away! If you have decided today to accept Christ and repent of your sins, I urge you to contact me and let me know any guidance that you need. My contact information is at the end of the book.

CHAPTER 13

Did the Nephilim (Giants) of Genesis Die in the Great Flood?

There is a lot of controversy around the existence and origin of the Nephilim. The Hebrew word *nefilim* is sometimes directly translated as "giants." In Genesis chapter 6, we read the following text:

> When man began to multiply on the face of the land and daughters were born to them, the sons of God saw that the daughters of man were attractive. And they took as their wives any they chose. Then the Lord said, "My Spirit shall not abide in man forever, for he is flesh: his days shall be 120 years." The Nephilim were on the earth in those days, and also afterward, when the sons of God came in to the daughters of man and they bore children to them. These were the mighty men who were of old, the men of renown. (Gen. 6:1–4 KJV)

Details about the Great Flood You Never Were Told

I suggest at this point we read on in pursuit of discovery in God's Word.

> The flood continued forty days on the earth. The waters increased and bore up the ark, and it rose high above the earth. The waters prevailed and increased greatly on the earth, and the ark floated on the face of the waters. And the waters prevailed so mightily on the earth that all the high mountains under the whole heaven were covered. The waters prevailed above the mountains, covering them fifteen cubits deep. And all flesh died that moved on the earth, birds, livestock, beasts, all swarming creatures that swarm on the earth, and all mankind. Everything on the dry land in whose nostrils was the breath of life died. He blotted out every living thing that was on the face of the ground, man and animals and creeping things and birds of the heavens. They were blotted out from the earth. Only Noah was left, and those who were with him in the ark. And the waters prevailed on the earth 150 days. (Gen. 7:17–30 ESV)

Verse 21–23 clearly states that all flesh died that moved on the earth. When God says all that is exactly what he means. This includes giants. In verse 20, we are told that the water was over 22.5 feet above the highest mountain. The highest mountain in the world is Mt. Everest, which is 29,032 feet high. So we add the 22.5 feet of water above Mt. Everest the water on the earth was 29,054.5 feet deep. Since the rain fell from heaven and the fountains of the earth for forty days and nights, the water was rising at 726.37 feet per day, which means it was raining 302.65 feet per day or 12.61 feet of rain per hour or 2.10 inches of rain per minute. Let us do some calculations. The largest mammals on the earth at that time being the Giraffe growing up to twenty feet high and the largest elephant being around thirteen feet high would have been easily drowned within the first two hours of rainfall if they were on flat land and I imagine they were. I will let you do any other calculations that you'd like. Remember that any fishing boat or boats that we know of that were historically in existence during the time of Noah would have been sunk by the pure magnitude of that storm. Now that we have estimated the rate of rainfall during the forty days that God sent the rain and the water we realize that the ark remained afloat over 3.5 months or 110 days after the rain stopped.

I think it is extremely important to examine the fruit of God's Word at this point as it pertains to the flood and what discoveries are to be made. To do that let's move forward to Genesis chapter 8.

> But God remembered Noah and all the beasts and all the livestock that were with him in the ark. And God made a wind blow over the earth, and the waters subsided. The *fountains of the deep and the windows of the heavens were closed,* the rain from the heavens was restrained, and the waters receded from the earth continually. At the end of 150 days, the waters *had abated,* and in the seventh month, on the seventeenth day of the month, the ark came to rest on the mountains of Ararat. And the waters continued to abate until the tenth month; in the tenth month, on the first day of the month, the tops of the mountains were seen. At the end of forty days, Noah opened the window of the ark that he had made and sent forth a raven. It went to and fro until the waters were dried up from the earth. Then he sent forth a dove from him, to see if the waters had subsided from the face of the ground. But the dove found no place to set her foot, and she returned to him to the ark, for the waters were still on the

face of the whole earth. So he put out his hand and took her and brought her into the ark with him. He waited another seven days, and again he sent forth the dove out of the ark. And the dove came back to him in the evening, and behold, in her mouth was a freshly plucked olive leaf. So Noah knew that the waters had subsided from the earth. Then he waited another seven days and sent forth the dove, and she did not return to him anymore. In the six hundred and first year, in the first month, the first day of the month, the waters were dried from off the earth. And Noah removed the covering of the ark and looked, and behold, the face of the ground was dry. In the second month, on the twenty-seventh day of the month, the earth had dried out. Then God said to Noah, "Go out from the ark, you and your wife, and your sons and your sons' wives with you. Bring out with you every living thing that is with you of all flesh—birds and animals and every creeping thing that creeps on the earth— that they may swarm on the earth, and be fruitful and multiply on the earth." So Noah went out, and his sons and his wife and his sons' wives with him. Every beast, every creeping thing, and every bird, everything that moves on the earth, went out by families from the ark. Then Noah built an altar to the LORD and took some of every clean animal and some of every clean bird and offered burnt offerings on the altar. And when the LORD smelled the pleasing aroma, the LORD said in his heart, "I will never again curse the ground because of man, for the intention of man's heart is evil from his youth. Neither will I ever again strike down every living creature as I have done. While the earth remains, seedtime and harvest,

cold and heat, summer and winter, day and
night, shall not cease. (Gen. 8:1–22 ESV)

I have often wondered and pondered things as I have read
Genesis 8:20–21:

> Then Noah built an altar to the LORD and
> took some of every clean animal and some of
> every clean bird and offered burnt offerings on
> the altar. And when the LORD smelled the pleas-
> ing aroma, the LORD said in his heart, "I will
> never again curse the ground because of man, for
> the intention of man's heart is evil from his youth.
> Neither will I ever again strike down every living
> creature as I have done. While the earth remains,
> seedtime and harvest, cold and heat, summer and
> winter, day and night, shall not cease."

Now Genesis 8:20–21 harbors some revelations as it pertains
to the essence of God. The first thing I noticed was three distinct
things that I had failed to recognize in my prior readings of the same
verses. The first hasty conclusion I came to was that when I read
verse 20, I thought well Noah just made several occupants of the
ark extinct! Because it clearly says he took "some" of every clean animal and "some" of every clean bird and offered them on the altar to
God. I said well Noah was only told to load up a male and female of
everything, so no matter which sex he sacrificed, it made that species
extinct. Then I said to myself, hold on here just a moment and think
about this more clearly by examining the facts. First, I think what
happened to me personally was that forty days and forty nights of
rain had brainwashed me. I didn't pause at all to think the boat was
aloft for a total of 150 days before coming to rest on the mountains
of Ararat which was "in the seventh month, on the seventeenth day
of the month" as it is written in Genesis 8:4 ESV.

Remembering that God had shut off the fountains of the deep
and the windows of heaven, then and only then did this great flood

begin subsiding. Subsiding doesn't mean the water had just vanished but it does mean the violence and the intensity of the storm had slowed down. God had shut down all sources of explosive water flow from the fountains of the earth and the heavens. The revelation of a time frame and occurrences is paramount to our understanding. Since the ark came to rest in the mountains of Ararat it is reasonable to use Mt. Everest as a point of reference. We have already discussed the fact that the Bible tells us that the tops of "all mountains" were not only covered but were under 22.5 feet of water themselves. This tells us that for Noah's ark to come to rest on the mountains of Ararat at approximately 16,854 feet the water level upon the earth would have dropped 12,200 feet using Mt. Everest as a point of reference as the highest mountain on the earth. Going back to the time frame we see in the seventh month Noah's ark came to rest and the scriptures go on to tell us that "And the waters continued to abate until the tenth month; in the tenth month, on the first day of the month, the tops of the mountains were seen" (Gen. 8:5 ESV).

We have now jumped three additional months in time before the tops of the other mountains could be seen. So if we recap all of the time detailed to us in Genesis chapter 8, we see that the severity of the storm didn't cease for 150 days or *five months* at which time the ark came to rest on the mountains of Ararat which is described as the seventh month, in the tenth month or *three months* later mountain tops could be seen, we read where Noah turns a turtle dove lose three separate times seven days apart or a total of *twenty-one days*. When Noah removed the covering of the Ark in the *first month on the first day of the month*, he saw that the face of the ground was dry. Yet God did not call Noah to come out until the *second month, on the twenty-seventh day of the month, which added another twenty-seven days after Noah noted the face of the ground was dry*. If you are adding with me the numbers strongly indicate the Ark was not abandoned until a year had passed. Remember in the days of Noah a month was counted as thirty days. You may ask yourself, "Was Egypt, here before the flood?" For now, I say consider this. The entire landscape of the Giza Necropolis, including the pyramids and the Sphinx, shows erosion that some say suggests the area was once submerged by seawater. Archaeologist Sherif El Morsi's discovery of a petrified sample of a type of sea urchin proves beyond doubt the Great Flood indeed covered the entire world with water. So who built the Sphinx and the Pyramids? Of course, these types of things can perhaps be examined in another book.

I want to refer back to the depth of the great flood and how fast that water begins to recede once God subdued the storm. We know that God's Word states the waters were 22.5 feet above the mountain peaks so we do our calculations with the height of Mt. Everest plus 22.5 feet.

Mt. Everest including the 22.5 of water above its highest point = 29,054.5 feet

The mountains of Ararat = 16,854 feet

Since the ark was adrift until the fifth month, a simple calculation tells us that the water had abated 12,200.5 feet for the Ark to rest upon its mountain at an elevation of 16,854 feet. So that tells us that the water receded at a rate of 2,440.10 feet per month. At this rate of abatement, it would take 11.9 months for the water to recede to ground level.

So this time element calms my fears of Noah's altar sacrifices to God would make some species extinct. Sheep, goats, and doves were used for sacrifice. Since sheep and goats are pregnant on average 150 days then both species could give birth during this journey. Lambs or ewes will give birth to one to three lambs at each birthing event while the goats will bear two kids per pregnancy. Doves usually lay one or two eggs and incubate them for fourteen to twenty nights while the male incubates them during the day. Doves will raise up to six broods per year. So there were more than enough animals for sacrifice. As you recall, this is one of the three revelations I saw in just Genesis 8:20–21. The second thing was that we are told that God can "smell" because when Noah offered up the burnt offerings we see that the smell was a pleasing aroma to God. Thirdly, God had remorse that he had destroyed all of the creatures mentioning that man was evil from his youth. Therefore we see that not only did God regret creating man "And it repented the LORD that he had made man on the earth, and it grieved him at his heart" (Gen. 6:6 KJV), he also regretted taking the lives of innocent creatures as well.

This brings us back to the giants or the Nephilim. Yes, they were here before the flood and after the flood, but not because they survived the great flood.

> The Nephilim were on the earth in those days, *and also afterward*, when the sons of God came into the daughters of man and they bore children to them. These were the mighty men who were of old, the men of renown." As we can see "and also afterward" the great flood the sons of God came again into the daughters of man. (Gen. 6:1–4 KJV)

The account of the reappearance is revealed in Numbers chapter 13.

> So they went up, and searched the land from the wilderness of Zin unto Rehob, as men come to Hamath. And they ascended by the south, and came unto Hebron; where Ahiman, Sheshai, and Talmai, the children of Anak, were. (Now Hebron was built seven years before Zoan in Egypt.) And they came unto the brook of Eshcol, and cut down from thence a branch with one cluster of grapes, and they bare it between two upon a staff; and they brought of the pomegranates, and of the figs. The place was called the brook Eshcol, because of the cluster of grapes which the children of Israel cut down from thence. And they returned from searching of the land after forty days. And they went and came to Moses, and to Aaron, and to all the congregation of the children of Israel, unto the wilderness of Paran, to Kadesh; and brought back word unto

them, and unto all the congregation, and shewed
them the fruit of the land. And they told him,
and said, We came unto the land whither thou
sentest us, and surely it floweth with milk and
honey; and this is the fruit of it. Nevertheless the
people be strong that dwell in the land, and the
cities are walled, and very great: and moreover we
saw the children of Anak there. The Amalekites
dwell in the land of the south: and the Hittites,
and the Jebusites, and the Amorites, dwell in the
mountains: and the Canaanites dwell by the sea,
and by the coast of Jordan. And Caleb stilled
the people before Moses, and said, Let us go up
at once, and possess it; for we are well able to
overcome it. But the men that went up with him
said, We be not able to go up against the people;
for they are stronger than we. And they brought
up an evil report of the land which they had
searched unto the children of Israel, saying, The
land, through which we have gone to search it, is
a land that eateth up the inhabitants thereof; and
all the people that we saw in it are men of a great
stature. And there we saw the giants, the sons of
Anak, which come of the giants: and we were in
our own sight as grasshoppers, and so we were in
their sight. (Num. 13:21–33 KJV)

Since the sons of God never perished because they are eternal,
they revisited the daughters of man.

CHAPTER 14

Is Overeating a Sin?

These are things that you will seldom if ever hear a sermon about in church. Nevertheless, most of these are noted as problematic, and they are all recognized by mankind as eating disorders! More than likely, you will hear sermons about the sinfulness of drug addiction, alcohol addiction, and sexual immorality all of which have enslaved mankind. You may be thinking gluttony isn't rated up there with those other "bad things," because most people think that way. In other words, why don't we want to talk about certain things that could or should be considered a sin? Let's look to God for all understanding and his word to grasp the truth about this matter.

First of all, Christ has called us to be holy. "Because it is, Be ye holy; for I am holy" (1 Peter 1:16 KJV). He has also told us, "If you love me keep my commandments" (John 14:15 ESV). Then we beg the question where has God spoken about my appetite in the Bible? Let's start here, "And put a knife to your throat if you are given to appetite" (Prov. 23:2 ESV). God then tells us how to do this, "For the grace of God has appeared that offers salvation to all people. It teaches us to say 'no' to ungodliness and worldly passions, and to live self-controlled, upright and godly lives in this present age" (Titus 2:11–12 NIV). So the Lord expects us to practice and exhibit self-control in all things. Paul talked about this as he preached at Corinth. "But I discipline my body and keep it under control, lest after preaching to others I myself should be disqualified" (1 Cor. 9:27 ESV).

Now the question we pondered before is reintroduced again. That question would be but gluttony isn't condemned like the addiction to alcohol, is it? The answer according to the scriptures is yes. "Hear, my son, and be wise, and direct your heart in the way. Be not among drunkards or among gluttonous eaters of meat for the drunkard and the glutton will come to poverty, and slumber will clothe them with rags" (Prov. 23:19–21 ESV). Therefore, to God, a drunkard and a glutton's sin are equal. Some people say that they have tried many diets and can't lose weight. This remark is weighing in on the other spectrum of this issue. This isn't about what you eat; it is about eating out of control or gluttony. We also read that has given everyone the power to overcome. "For God gave us a spirit not of fear but of power and love and self-control" (2 Tim. 1:7 ESV). God not only gave us two ears but he gave us two eyes, legs, arms, and feet for reasons other than to travel. "But be ye doers of the word, and not hearers only, deceiving your own selves" (James 1:22 KJV). God finally tells us that if we have no self-control then we are pretty much without hope. "A man without self-control is like a city broken into and left without walls" (Prov. 25:28 ESV). Let us constantly go to prayer to God asking for the strength to utilize our power and free will and self-control so we can honor him. "What? know ye not that your body is the temple of the Holy Ghost which is in you, which ye have of God, and ye are not your own? For ye are bought with a price: therefore glorify God in your body, and in your spirit, which are God's" (1 Cor. 6:19–20 KJV).

Does God Speak to Us through Our Conscience?

Most people agree that our conscience is the voice inside us that guides and tells us what we should and shouldn't do. The voice that tells us what is right and what is wrong. People have different opinions about what the conscience is and how we acquired it. Our conscience no doubt is part of our human psyche. The word *conscience* itself is made up of two words—*con* and *science*. *Science* comes from the Latin word *scire*, meaning "knowledge." *Con* means "with," so when combined with *science*, both indicate that we are thinking with knowledge. With this in mind, let us go to the Word of God and see what God has to say about its source and for more discovery.

> For when Gentiles, who do not have the law, by nature do what the law requires, they are a law to themselves, even though they do not have the law. They show that the work of the law is written on their hearts, while their conscience also bears witness, and their conflicting thoughts accuse or even excuse them. (Rom. 2:14–15 ESV)

This scripture tells us that we have inherited our conscience naturally, and it bears witness to the truth.

> But this I confess to you, that according to the Way, which they call a sect, I worship the God of our fathers, believing everything laid down by the Law and written in the Prophets, having a hope in God, which these men themselves accept, that there will be a resurrection of both the just and the unjust. So I always take pains to have a clear conscience toward both God and man. (Acts 24:14–16 ESV)

Paul in this writing states he "takes pain to have a clear conscience toward God and man." In other words, Paul wants to do what is decent, honest, and holy to both God and man. Scripture tells us that our conscience can be defiled or poisoned.

> Yet for us there is one God, the Father, from whom are all things and for whom we exist, and one Lord, Jesus Christ, through whom are all things and through whom we exist. However, not

all possess this knowledge. But some, through former association with idols, eat food as really offered to an idol, and their conscience, being weak, is defiled. (1 Cor. 8:6–7 ESV)

Pray for us: for we trust we have a good conscience, in all things willing to live honestly. (Heb. 13:18 KJV)

The word *conscience* is used twenty-nine times in the New Testament. All that I read in God's Word stresses that it is something that he gave to us but it is not God himself talking to us. God is unchanging. Our conscience on the other hand can be twisted, tarnished, and seared by our own free will. Sometimes, I think we run the moral red light of the conscience so much that is when we sear it. When that feeling of guilt or remorse that we once felt just dissolves away. At times, God will challenge us in an attempt to reform our conscience but he doesn't take away our free will. We are still the ones that must take the steps to find our true north on our compass of morality.

CHAPTER 15

What Happened to the Twelve Apostles of Jesus Christ?

It has been said that the apostles were all common people of their day. However, all of them had found favored by God, even Judas, who would betray Jesus at the appointed time. The apostles were each unique in their own way. We must realize that we can only see them from the outside and are unable to see their hearts as God would do. These twelve men had what many would consider the impossible dream. That was to teach the gospel to every creature just as instructed in Mark 16:15 KJV: "And he said unto them, Go ye into all the world, and preach the gospel to every creature." They did exactly what Jesus had commanded them to do. In the brutal empire of Rome where Christians were slaughtered for sport by being fed to wild beasts and burned alive, an amazing transformation occurred. In less than three hundred years, the majority of the Roman Empire would be followers of the Christian faith. This road was not easy from the very beginning which leaves us with a great question of discovery and curiosity. How did the disciples die and what happened to them?

Many wonder how the twelve apostles died, but the New Testament tells of the fate of only two of the apostles: Judas, who betrayed Jesus and then went out and hanged himself, and James the son of Zebedee, who was executed by Herod about AD 44. "About that time Herod the king laid violent hands on some who belonged to the church. He killed James the brother of John with the sword" (Acts 12:1–2 ESV).

The scriptures do not reveal how the other apostles died, however, due to both legend and some Jewish historians we do have some idea as to how they met their end. Their bold allegiance to witness the truth of the Lord Jesus Christ brought about their violent deaths. The following is not biblically supported and most is a matter of Christian tradition and ancient history.

Peter. Both Peter and Paul were executed Roman-style during the great persecution under Emperor Nero. Peter at his request was crucified upside down since he did not feel worthy to die in the manner as his Lord Jesus.

Paul. It is expected that Paul died shortly aft his letter to Timothy while in prison in Rome. Paul knew he was going to be put to death soon.

> For I am already being poured out as a drink offering, and the Thomas took the Gospel to India and was put to death by a spear. Time of my departure has come. I have fought the good fight, I have finished the race, I have kept the faith. Henceforth there is laid up for me the crown of righteousness, which the Lord, the righteous judge, will award to me on that day, and not only to me but also to all who have loved his appearing. (2 Tim. 4:6–8 ESV)

Tradition said Paul was beheaded by Nero very likely in AD 67 or AD 68.

John. John in general is thought to be the only apostle that died of natural causes. John had taken care of Mary the mother of Jesus in his home. He was the leader of the church in the Ephesus area. John was exiled to the island of Patmos where he wrote Revelation. Some of the early Latin legends have him escaping unhurt after being cast into boiling oil at Rome.

Thomas. According to Christian tradition, Thomas was probably most active in the area east of Syria, but it is believed that he preached as far as India. It was there where it is said that he was pierced and killed by Hindu priests of Kali.

Andrew. Christian tradition records that Andrew went to the Soviet Union. It is believed that he preached in Asia Minor, modern-day Turkey, and in Greece, where he is said to have been crucified on an X-shaped cross in Greece. It is said he hung on that cross for two days, preaching to onlookers until he died.

Philip. Tradition records that Philip had a ministry in Carthage in North Africa and then Asia Minor where he converted the wife of a Roman proconsul. In retaliation, the proconsul had Philip arrested and cruelly put to death. Phillip preached in Greece, Syria, and Turkey, and finally in Egypt. There are conflicting versions of his death in Edessa, Turkey. One story is that he was crucified and the other says that he was clubbed or beaten to death. His remains are buried in a crypt in Rome.

Matthew. The tax collector and writer of a Gospel ministered in Persia and Ethiopia. Some of the oldest reports say he was not martyred while others say he was stabbed to death in Ethiopia.

Bartholomew. According to Christian tradition, Bartholomew went to India with Thomas, back to Armenia, and also to Ethiopia and Southern Arabia. There are various accounts of how he met his death as a martyr for the gospel. One says that he was killed by being flogged to death by a whip in Armenia.

James. The son of Alpheus is one of at least three James referred to in the New Testament. There is some confusion as to which is which, but this James is reckoned to have ministered in Syria. The Jewish historian Josephus reported that he was stoned and then clubbed to death.

Simon the Zealot. So the story goes, ministered in Persia (modern-day Iran) and was killed after refusing to sacrifice to the sun god. The method of death is in disagreement. One said he was crucified and the other killed by the sword.

Judas Iscariot. Judas Iscariot was a disciple and one of the original twelve apostles of Jesus Christ. According to all four canonical gospels, Judas betrayed Jesus to the Sanhedrin in the garden of Gethsemane by kissing him and addressing him as "rabbi" to reveal his identity in the darkness to the crowd who had come to arrest him. There has been much debate concerning Judas and Acts 1:18 which respectfully says, "Now this man acquired a field with the reward of his wickedness, and falling headlong he burst open in the middle and all his bowels gushed out." In my opinion, Matthew 27:3–10 ESV explains away any confusion.

> Then when Judas, his betrayer, saw that Jesus was condemned, he changed his mind and brought back the thirty pieces of silver to the chief priests and the elders, saying, "I have sinned by betraying innocent blood." They said, "What is that to us? See to it yourself." And throwing down the pieces of silver into the temple, he departed, and he went and hanged himself. But the chief priests, taking the pieces of silver, said, "It is not lawful to put them into the treasury, since it is blood money."

So they took counsel and bought with them the potter's field as a burial place for strangers. Therefore, that field has been called the Field of Blood to this day. Then was fulfilled what had been spoken by the prophet Jeremiah, saying, "And they took the thirty pieces of silver, the price of him on whom a price had been set by some of the sons of Israel, and they gave them for the potter's field, as the Lord directed me." Both the gospels and Luke and John state when Judas was overtaken by Satan. "Then after he had taken the morsel, Satan entered into him. Jesus said to him, "What you are going to do, do quickly" (John 13:27 ESV).

Matthias. Matthias was the apostle chosen to replace Judas.

> And they put forward two, Joseph called Barsabbas, who was also called Justus, and Matthias. And they prayed and said, "You, Lord,

> who know the hearts of all, show which one of these two you have chosen to take the place in this ministry and apostleship from which Judas turned aside to go to his own place. And they cast lots for them, and the lot fell on Matthias, and he was numbered with the eleven apostles. (Acts 1:23–26 ESV)

Matthias, often confused with the apostle Matthew, who was chosen to replace Judas Iscariot, has often been confused with the apostle Matthew. Some accounts note his death in Ethiopia while other accounts note his death in Cappadocia (eastern Turkey). Greek tradition states that he Christianized Cappadocia, a mountainous district now in central Turkey, later journeying to the region about the Caspian Sea, where he was martyred by crucifixion and, according to other legends, chopped apart.

Thaddeus. He is recorded in most traditions as traveling to Persia with Simon the Zealot and being martyred there. The actual means of death is unknown. According to Catholicism, Thaddaeus was also known as St. Jude. Biblical scholars agree he was the son of Clopas and his mother Mary was the Virgin Mary's cousin; therefore, he was a relative of Jesus Christ.

C H A P T E R   16

What Is the Name of God?

Since a third of the earth's population identifies themselves as Christians, the Holy Bible is the foundation of over 2.5 billion people's religion. A huge part of western culture was influenced by the Bible. A large portion of the earth's population is at least somewhat familiar with the Bible, its stories, and even one or more verses that seem to demand their attention. Even though the Bible has been studied since its creation and scholars by the scores have spent their entire lives not only studying its contents but searching for answers to mysteries as well. One of those is what is the true name of God?

When asked what God's name is, people usually in general will just say simply "God," while others may say that it is Jesus Christ since the Father and the Son are one simultaneously. Others will say that the divine name was either hidden from mankind or that it is forbidden to speak. Still, others will claim it is "Yahweh." The people in camps two and three would be the closest according to the Old Testament where God is actually spoken of by name. In English Bibles, the use of God's name is usually translated as "Lord" in all capital letters to signify when God's name was used as opposed to His various titles and epithets.

In Hebrew, God's name was written using the consonants YHWH. It is from these letters that modern scholars get the name "Yahweh" as the most likely pronunciation. Unfortunately, no one knows whether or not this is the correct pronunciation. Ancient

Hebrew did not have vowels, and it was taboo to speak the divine name. As such, the actual pronunciation of YHWH was slowly lost. Most people believe that it was pronounced "Yahweh," but no one can confirm that for certain. There are several references to God and what he and others called him in the Bible especially in the Old Testament. "And God spake unto Moses, and said unto him, I am the Lord: And I appeared unto Abraham, unto Isaac, and unto Jacob, by *the name of God Almighty*, but by *my name JEHOVAH* was I not known to them" (Exod. 6:2–3 KJV). In this passage, God says that "I am the Lord" and goes on to tell Moses that he was known as "God Almighty" to Abraham, Isaac, and Jacob. King David refers to God in three different ways just in six verses.

> O my God, make them like a wheel; as the stubble before the wind. As the fire burneth a wood, and as the flame setteth the mountains on fire; So persecute them with thy tempest, and make them afraid with thy storm. Fill their faces with shame; that they may seek thy name, O Lord. Let them be confounded and troubled for ever; yea, let them be put to shame, and perish: That men may know that thou, whose name alone is JEHOVAH, art the most high over all the earth. (Ps. 83:13–18 KJV)

In these six verses alone, David uses the names God, Lord, and Jehovah to make his requests and praises known. In Genesis 22:14 in the King James Version, we read, "And Abraham called the name of that place Jehovahjireh: as it is said to this day, In the mount of the Lord it shall be seen." Reading the same verse in the English Standard Version we discover the meaning of "Jehovahjireh." So Abraham called the name of that place, "The Lord will provide," as it is said to this day, "On the mount of the Lord it shall be provided. So the meaning of "Jehovahjireh" is "The Lord shall provide." In both versions, God is referred to as the Lord. In different scripture, we see God instructing his servants to refer to him as different things in particular."

When God exclaims who he is he proclaims some other attributes as well.

> He said, But I will be with you, and this shall be the sign for you, that I have sent you: when you have brought the people out of Egypt, you shall serve God on this mountain." Then Moses said to God, "If I come to the people of Israel and say to them, 'The God of your fathers has sent me to you,' and they ask me, 'What is his name?' what shall I say to them?" God said to Moses, "I AM WHO I AM." And he said, "Say this to the people of Israel: I AM has sent me to you." (Exod. 3:12–14 ESV)

We can tell by these verses that God does not allow anyone to place words in his mouth. His expression of "I Am Who I Am" perhaps is a statement of fact. That fact is that his name or nature cannot be conceived or processed by a mere name. My name is Mark, yet that name doesn't define who I am, who I've been, or what I will become. If "I Am" was to give himself a name that was expressive of his nature and existence, it would be impossible to do so in any tongue or language. What name would you give to an existence without beginning or end? Remember forever is defined as "for all future time; for always, continually."

Even the word *forever* started somewhere. God created all reference points of being, including time itself. Before there was even a measurement of time like the sundial God gave us what I refer to as time in the trees or the seasons. Day and night. Our perception of everything is based upon a beginning and an end. This is why God also declared "I am Alpha and Omega, the beginning and the end, the first and the last" (Rev. 22:13 KJV). When Jesus's disciples asked him how to pray, he did not call out the name of God. He did say that his name was "hallowed" or holy.

> After this manner therefore pray ye: Our
> Father which art in heaven, Hallowed be thy
> name. Thy kingdom come, Thy will be done in
> earth, as it is in heaven. Give us this day our daily
> bread. And forgive us our debts, as we forgive
> our debtors. And lead us not into temptation but
> deliver us from evil: For thine is the kingdom,
> and the power, and the glory, forever. Amen.
> (Matt. 6:9–13 KJV)

Jesus goes on in verses 14 and 15 to take about the importance of forgiveness. "For if ye forgive men their trespasses, your heavenly Father will also forgive you: But if ye forgive not men their trespasses, neither will your Father forgive your trespasses" (Matt. 6:14–15 KJV). The last two times Jesus calls out to the father is while he suffered on Calvary: "And at the ninth hour Jesus cried with a loud voice, 'Eloi, Eloi, lema sabachthani?' which means, 'My God, my God, why have you forsaken me?'" (Mark 15:34 ESV). With the final breath of Jesus's earthy existence in the body of a man he said, "And when Jesus had cried with a loud voice, he said, Father, into thy hands I commend my spirit: and having said thus, he gave up the ghost" (Luke 23:46 KJV). In conclusion, I think it is evident through these scriptures we can see and understand the name of God is intangible.

Does God Have a Soul?

On the sixth day of creation, we see the first mention of a soul in the Bible when God created Adam. "Then God said, 'Let us make man in our image, after our likeness. And let them have dominion over the fish of the sea and over the birds of the heavens and over the livestock and over all the earth and over every creeping thing that creeps on the earth'" (Gen. 1:26 ESV). The words "in our image" and "after our likeness" should be pondered to grasp what the scriptures are saying! "And the Lord God formed man of the dust of the ground, and breathed into his nostrils the breath of life, and man became a living soul" (Gen. 2:7 KJV). Nothing in all of creation that God had produced including all the creatures of the earth was made his image but man. The Psalmist wrote, "For God alone, O my soul, wait in silence, for my hope is from him" (Ps. 62:5 ESV). "Bless the Lord, O my soul! O Lord my God, you are very great! You are clothed with splendor and majesty" (Ps. 104:1 ESV). The evidence that shows and demonstrates that God has a soul is in these scriptures. "And I set my tabernacle among you: *and my soul* shall not abhor you" (Lev. 26:11 KJV). In Leviticus, he tells the people that "his soul" shall not abhor or hate them, which is stark evidence of God's emotions. "I will rejoice in doing them good, and I will plant them in this land in faithfulness, with all my heart *and all my soul*" (Jer. 32:41 KJV). Again, we see that God's emotions are evident again since he says that he rejoices in doing good and that his pledge of faithfulness is done with both his heart and soul. "And they put away the strange gods from among them, and served the Lord: and his soul was grieved for the misery of Israel" (Judges 10:16 ESV). God's emotions once again showed up in this verse as he was grieved over the misery or suffering of Israel. Some will deny that God has a soul, however, we must accept God's Word as the final authority. This is regardless of what scholars or anything man would say.

CHAPTER 17

Who Was Melchizedek?

Many people have either never heard a sermon about Melchizedek or if they ever heard anything it was brief and without any depth or discussion about who he was. This priest and king called Melchizedek is one of the great mysteries of the Bible and this one fascinates me. When I read that Jesus is mentioned as being forever in the priesthood of Melchizedek, I begin a journey into a web of mystery and records that I vigorously pursued in search of a better understanding of him calling on God for spiritual guidance. I begin in Genesis 14:17–20,

> After his return from the defeat of Chedorlaomer and the kings who were with him, the king of Sodom went out to meet him at the Valley of Shaveh (that is, the King's Valley). And Melchizedek king of Salem brought out bread and wine. (He was priest of God Most High.) And he blessed him and said, "Blessed be Abram by God Most High, Possessor of heaven and earth; and blessed be God Most High, who has delivered your enemies into your hand!"

This is the first occurrence of Melchizedek in the Old Testament. He suddenly appears in the middle of a narrative where Abram is coming from battle and he blesses him. Abram honored Melchizedek by giving him one-tenth of the plunder of battle, or a tithe. We see that he is King of Salem (which would later become Jerusalem) and a priest of God Most High and priest of God most high. The fact that it is stated that he is both King and Priest becomes contrary to biblical tradition and is problematic. In the following passage of scripture, we read why.

> But when he was strong, he grew proud, to his destruction. For he was unfaithful to the LORD his God and entered the temple of the LORD to burn incense on the altar of incense. But Azariah the priest went in after him, with eighty priests of the LORD who were men of valor, and they withstood King Uzziah and said to him, "It is not for you, Uzziah, to burn incense to the LORD, but for the priests, the sons of Aaron, who are consecrated to burn incense. Go out of the sanctuary, for you have done wrong, and it will bring you no honor from the LORD God." Then Uzziah was angry. Now he had a censer in his hand to burn incense, and when he became angry with the priests, leprosy broke out on his forehead in the presence of the priests in the house of the LORD, by the altar of incense. And Azariah the chief priest and all the priests looked at him, and behold, he was leprous in his forehead! And they rushed him out quickly, and he himself hurried to go out, because the LORD had struck him. And King Uzziah was a leper to the day of his death, and being a leper lived in a separate house, for he was excluded from the house of the LORD. And Jotham his son was over the king's household, governing the people of the land. Now the rest of the acts of Uzziah, from first to last, Isaiah the prophet the son of Amoz wrote. And Uzziah

slept with his fathers, and they buried him with his fathers in the burial field that belonged to the kings, for they said, "He is a leper." And Jotham his son reigned in his place. (Chron. 26:16–23 ESV)

We can see that a king of Israel cannot be both king and priest since we see that any king that tries to be a priest is smitten by the Lord. The only time a King could be a priest in Judaism was during the time of the Maccabees. The second place in the Old Testament we see reference to Melchizedek is in Psalms. "The LORD has sworn and will not change his mind, "You are a priest forever after the order of Melchizedek" (Ps. 110:4 ESV). David connects Melchizedek to Jesus the Messiah. In Hebrews 7:17 (ESV), it is written, "For it is witnessed of him, 'You are a priest forever, after the order of Melchizedek.'" Melchizedek has no genealogy, no reference of a birth.

Without father, without mother, without descent, having neither beginning of days, nor end of life; but made like unto the Son of God; abideth a priest continually. Now consider how great this man was, unto whom even the patriarch Abraham gave the tenth of the spoils. And verily they that are of the sons of Levi, who receive the office of the priesthood, have a commandment to take tithes of the people according to the law, that is, of their brethren, though they come out of the loins of Abraham: But he whose descent is not counted from them received tithes of Abraham, and blessed him that had the promises. And without all contradiction the less is blessed of the better. (Heb. 7:3–7 KJV)

He is a priest of God during a time when there were very few godly men. Some biblical scholars have wondered if Melchizedek could have been a manifestation of Jesus before the Nativity. However, the references made in Hebrews, stating that Jesus "is a priest after the order of Melchizedek," would deny that could be possible. I think the scriptures bear witness that Melchizedek is no ordinary man and strikes a comparison of him and Jesus in one verse. "Without father, without mother, without descent, having neither beginning of days, nor end of life; but made like unto the Son of God; abideth a priest continually" (Heb. 7:3 KJV). Since Melchizedek had no mother, no father, no beginning of days, nor end of life one can safely say his existence is eternal and he is a supernatural being. He is recognized centuries apart by Abraham, King David, and the author of Hebrews. Remember, it is written, he is without end of life so his appearance in the scriptures which span centuries is not due to physical longevity. This is the extent of what the Holy Bible tells us about Melchizedek. Melchizedek does appear in other religions. Reference to him has been found in the Dead Sea Scrolls in Cave 11. 11Q13, which mentions Melchizedek as leader of God's angels in a war in heaven against the angels of darkness instead of the more familiar Archangel Michael. Based upon the three references to him in the Holy Bible, only my conclusion is that Melchizedek was an eternal creation of God, who was special, and he had been given the power to do the will of God.

What Happened to the Garden of Eden?

There is a lot of theories and pure speculation regarding the whereabouts of the garden of Eden. Where was it originally located and where is it now? The biblical reference to its location is not specific, however, the scripture does give us reference points.

> A river flowed out of Eden to water the garden, and there it divided and became four rivers. The name of the first is the Pishon. It is the one that flowed around the whole land of Havilah, where there is gold. And the gold of that land is good; bdellium and onyx stone are there. The name of the second river is the Gihon. It is the one that flowed around the whole land of Cush. And the name of the third river is the Tigris, which flows east of Assyria. And the fourth river is the Euphrates. (Gen. 2:10–14 NIV)

Some scholars do not consider the garden of Eden real at all, however, due to the geographical description in the Bible, although no one can be certain its location seems to be at the head of the Persian Gulf, in southern Mesopotamia, which is now Iraq. This is where the Tigris and the Euphrates rivers run into the sea and in Armenia. Therefore, to think it didn't exist at all when there are geographical reference points written thousands of years ago that still exist today escapes all logic.

Although we don't have a biblical GPS, we have definitive reference points because the Bible gives us the names of the rivers that ran through the garden. The Pishon and Gihon rivers are not seen on any modern maps but the presence of Eden was on maps dating back to the 1400s. According to historical accounts in 1498, Christopher Columbus was horrified as his ship sailed up the water of the Orinoco River. Columbus thought that he was about to enter the garden of Eden, which would result in his certain death. This area is now known as present-day Venezuela. Today, our maps now complete, it seems that Eden has vanished without a trace.

Here is the scripture where we will find some answers.

> And the LORD God planted a garden in Eden, in the east, and there he put the man whom he had formed. And out of the ground the LORD God made to spring up every tree that is pleasant to the sight and good for food. The tree of life was in the midst of the garden, and the tree of the knowledge of good and evil. A river flowed out of Eden to water the garden, and there it divided and became four rivers. The name of the first is the Pishon. It is the one that flowed around the whole land of Havilah, where there is gold. And the gold of that land is good; bdellium and onyx stone are there. The name of the second river is the Gihon. It is the one that flowed around the whole land of Cush. And the name of the third river is the Tigris, which flows east of Assyria. And the fourth river is the Euphrates. The LORD God took the man and put him in the garden of Eden to work it and keep it. And the LORD God commanded the man, saying, "You may surely eat of

every tree of the garden, but of the tree of the knowledge of good and evil you shall not eat, for in the day that you eat of it you shall surely die." Then the LORD God said, "It is not good that the man should be alone; I will make him a helper fit for him." Now out of the ground the LORD God had formed every beast of the field and every bird of the heavens and brought them to the man to see what he would call them. And whatever the man called every living creature, that was its name. The man gave names to all livestock and to the birds of the heavens and to every beast of the field. But for Adam there was not found a helper fit for him. So the LORD God caused a deep sleep to fall upon the man, and while he slept took one of his ribs and closed up its place with flesh. And the rib that the LORD God had taken from the man he made into a woman and brought her to the man. Then the man said, "This at last is bone of my bones and flesh of my flesh; she shall be called Woman, because she was taken out of Man. (Gen. 2:8–23 ESV)

We understand Eden is not just made up of a garden. Eden, in fact, is a much larger piece of land. The one thing that makes "the garden of Eden" so special is that God personally planted the garden "eastward" in Eden, and it's right in the midst of the garden was the tree of life and the tree of good and evil. One of the trees harnessed the power of perpetual life without end, which was the tree of life and the other tree held the power of death, the tree of good and evil.

Many have questioned why the tree of good and evil was even placed in the garden if just this one tree could become the downfall of man. We must examine the fact that God had placed Adam and Eve in the garden to tend it. *Tend* means "to take care of or be in charge of someone or something." God didn't ask Adam to tend the garden he told him to tend it. At this point, neither Adam nor Eve had freedom of choice. Without the knowledge of evil and good, it would be impossible for them to make a judgment call or have discernment. This is the reason the tree of good and evil was placed there. They did not know what temptation was until Eve was confronted by Satan in the form of a serpent.

What has happened to the original garden of Eden and her fate isn't answered biblically. For me to say I know exactly or even have a clue would be less than truthful. I don't know the answer to that nor does anyone else with a true source of truth which is God's Word. I have even been asked what happened to the cherubim and the flaming sword God placed at the East point of the garden after he drove out Adam and Eve. All I know about that is what is said in Genesis 3:4 (NIV), "After he drove the man out, he placed on the east side of the Garden of Eden cherubim and a flaming sword flashing back and forth to guard the way to the tree of life." God is silent about how, and when the angel was relieved of duty from guarding the tree of life.

Although two of the rivers mentioned in Genesis have vanished Tigris and Euphrates Rivers have survived until the present day. These two rivers survived because of the way God designed them. They are cut into deep and permanent beds of rock. Their courses have undergone very little change during the beginning of time. Perhaps this is God's way of leaving a clue as to be evidence that the garden of Eden did, in fact, exist. We can logically conclude that the rest of the remains of the garden of Eden was swept away without a trace during the Great Flood of Noah.

CHAPTER 19

What Does the Bible Say About Cremation?

The first time we see any use of Cremation is in the book of Joshua.

In Joshua 7:16–26, we see the punishment of a soldier and his family for disobeying God.

Early the next morning, Joshua had Israel come forward by tribes, and Judah was chosen. The clans of Judah came forward, and the Zerahites were chosen. He had the clan of the Zerahites come forward by families, and Zimri was chosen. Joshua had his family come forward man by man, and Achan son of Karmi, the son of Zimri, the son of Zerah, of the tribe of Judah, was chosen.

Then Joshua said to Achan, "My son, give glory to the Lord, the God of Israel, and honor him. Tell me what you have done; do not hide it from me."

Achan replied, "It is true! I have sinned against the Lord, the God of Israel. This is what I have done: When I saw in the plunder a beautiful robe from Babylonia, two hundred shekels of silver and a bar of gold weighing fifty shekels, I coveted them and took them. They are hidden in the ground inside my tent, with the silver underneath."

So Joshua sent messengers, and they ran to the tent, and there it was, hidden in his tent, with the silver underneath. They took the things from the tent, brought them to Joshua and all the Israelites, and spread them out before the Lord.

Then Joshua, together with all Israel, took Achan son of Zerah, the silver, the robe, the gold bar, his sons and daughters, his cattle, donkeys and sheep, his tent and all that he had, to the Valley of Achor. Joshua said, "Why have you brought this trouble on us? The LORD will bring trouble on you today."

Then all Israel stoned him, and after they had stoned the rest, they *burned them*. Over Achan, they heaped up a large pile of rocks, which remains to this day. Then the LORD turned from his fierce anger. Therefore, that place has been called the Valley of Achor ever since.

Achan and his daughters suffered a gruesome death because Achan had taken the spoils of the war against Jericho after God had forbidden it. God had commanded the Israelites to destroy the entire city of Jericho because of its great sin. Only Rahab the harlot and her household were spared because she had hidden the Israelite spies. "And the city and all that is within it shall be devoted to the LORD for destruction. Only Rahab the prostitute and all who are with her in her house shall live, because she hid the messengers whom we sent" (Josh. 6:17 ESV). God further commanded that, unlike most victories when soldiers were allowed to take the spoils, the Israelites were to take nothing from Jericho. Everything in it was devoted to destruction. God warned that anyone taking spoils from Jericho would suffer and make the camp of Israel liable to destruction and bring trouble on it.

> But you, keep yourselves from the things devoted to destruction, lest when you have devoted them you take any of the devoted things and make the camp of Israel a thing for destruction and bring trouble upon it. But all silver and gold, and every vessel of bronze and iron, are holy to the LORD; they shall go into the treasury of the LORD. (Josh. 6:18–19 ESV)

By taking the gold and silver Achan stole from God. In this case, cremation was a means of cremation and a shameful end.

Another case of cremation in God's Word was in part due to the circumstances as we read the story in 1 Samuel.

> Now the Philistines fought against Israel: and the men of Israel fled from before the Philistines, and fell down slain in mount Gilboa. And the Philistines followed hard upon Saul and upon his sons; and the Philistines slew Jonathan, and Abinadab, and Melchishua, Saul's sons. And the battle went sore against Saul, and the archers hit him; and he was sore wounded of the archers. Then said Saul unto his armourbearer, Draw thy sword, and thrust me through therewith; lest these uncircumcised come and thrust me through, and abuse me. But his armourbearer would not; for he was sore afraid. Therefore Saul took a sword and fell upon it.
>
> And when his armourbearer saw that Saul was dead, he fell likewise upon his sword and died with him. So Saul died, and his three sons, and his armourbearer, and all his men, that same day together. And when the men of Israel that were on the other side of the valley, and they that were on the other side Jordan, saw that the men of Israel fled and that Saul and his sons were dead, they forsook the cities, and fled; and the Philistines came and dwelt in them. And it came to pass on the morrow when the Philistines came to strip the slain, that they found Saul and his three sons fallen in mount Gilboa. And they cut off his head, and stripped off his armor, and sent into the land of the Philistines round about, to publish it in the house of their idols, and among the people. And they put his armor in the house of Ashtaroth: and they fastened his body to the wall of Bethshan. And when the inhabitants of Jabeshgilead heard

of that which the Philistines had done to Saul; All the valiant men arose, and went all night, and took the body of Saul and the bodies of his sons from the wall of Bethshan, and came to Jabesh, and burnt them there. And they took their bones, and buried them under a tree at Jabesh, and fasted seven days. (1 Sam. 31:1–13 KJV)

Instead of obeying the Lord during his reign of Israel and turning to God for answers and strength concerning this great battle King Saul had searched out the witch of Endor to summon the spirit of the prophet Samuel. According to the Bible Samuel did rise up and immediately said to him, "Samuel said to Saul, 'Why have you disturbed me by bringing me up?'" (1 Sam. 28:15 NIV). Have you ever heard the expression "Don't disturb the dead"? Well, according to this verse, Samuel was not happy about being disturbed or woken up and he went on to tell King Saul that both he and his sons would be beheaded the next day and be with him.

We see in the book of Amos that cremation and the burning of human flesh is a punishment of the Lord.

Thus saith the LORD; For three transgressions of Moab, and for four, I will not turn away the punishment thereof; because he burned the bones of the king of Edom into lime: But I will send a fire upon Moab, and it shall devour the palaces of Kirioth: and Moab shall die with tumult, with shouting, and with the sound of the trumpet: And I will cut off the judge from the midst thereof, and will slay all the princes thereof with him, saith the LORD.

Thus saith the LORD; For three transgressions of Judah, and for four, I will not turn away the punishment thereof; because they have despised the law of the LORD, and have not kept his commandments, and their lies caused them to err, after the which their fathers have walked: But I will send a fire upon Judah, and it shall devour the palaces of Jerusalem. (Amos 2:1–5 KJV)

There is other evidence of cremations in scripture being a punishment that required the transgressors to be burned up with fire. The following incidents are a result of sins and they are cursed people. Here are two other examples.

If a man marries both a woman and her mother, it is wicked. Both he and they must be burned in the fire, so that no wickedness will be among you. (Lev. 20:14 NIV).

The Lord God has sworn by himself, declares the Lord, the God of hosts: I abhor the pride of Jacob and hate his strongholds, and I will deliver up the city and all that is in it." And if ten men remain in one house, they shall die. And when one's relative, the one who anoints him for burial, shall take him up to bring the bones out of the house, and shall say to him who is in the innermost parts of the house, "Is there still anyone with you?" he shall say, "No"; and he shall say, "Silence! We must not mention the name of the Lord. (Amos 6:8–10 ESV)

But you have done evil above all who were before you and have gone and made for yourself other gods and metal images, provoking me to anger, and have cast me behind your back, therefore behold, I will bring harm upon the house of Jeroboam and will cut off from Jeroboam every male, both bond and free in Israel, and will burn up the house of Jeroboam, as a man burns up dung until it is all gone. Anyone belonging to

> Jeroboam who dies in the city the dogs shall eat,
> and anyone who dies in the open country the
> birds of the heavens shall eat, for the LORD has
> spoken it. (1 Kings 14:9–11 ESV)

To remain unburied was considered shameful, even an indication of divine punishment, which we can see in the scriptures.

The word buried itself is found in 102 verses in the Bible in twenty-two books of the Bible, which is exactly a third of the Bible since the King James Version contains sixty-six books. For the Israel of old, burial in a tomb, cave, or in the ground was the common way to honor and dispose of a human body. Today, there is much controversy concerning burial and cremation. Some believe that cremation is a sin. There is a pagan belief that burning tends to purify the spirit and wards off evil spirits, which we know has no justification in the scriptures. As we have discussed there are conditional justifications of disposing of bodies in untraditional ways. One good example of this is the many wartime burials at sea, which have occurred in the past. Burial at sea is still possible today. The requirement of this to be carried out is that the individual had to be an active-duty member of the uniformed services or an honorably discharged veteran.

According to the Old Testament and New Testament, burial is the standard practice adopted for disposing of a dead body. Burial is not only a tradition but deep respect and reverence for the body. Otherwise, why would God himself bury someone?

> And the LORD said to him, "This is the land
> of which I swore to Abraham, to Isaac, and to
> Jacob, 'I will give it to your offspring.' I have let
> you see it with your eyes, but you shall not go
> over there." So Moses the servant of the LORD
> died there in the land of Moab, according to the
> word of the LORD, and he buried him in the val-
> ley in the land of Moab opposite Beth-peor; but
> no one knows the place of his burial to this day.
> (Deut. 34:4–6 ESV)

So what, as Christians, is our light that always leads our way? Of course, it is the living Word of God the Father and the Lord Jesus Christ who is the word. As Christians, we are also by definition are "Christ-like." There are many verses of scriptures that point to burial and our relationship with our faith and with our savior. "We were therefore buried with him through baptism into death so that, just as Christ was raised from the dead through the glory of the Father, we too may live a new life" (Rom. 6:4 NIV). We are to emulate the ways of Jesus just as he gave charge to his disciples before ascending into Heaven.

> And Jesus came and said to them, "All authority in heaven and on earth has been given to me. Go therefore and make disciples of all nations, baptizing them in the name of the Father and of the Son and of the Holy Spirit, teaching them to observe all that I have commanded you. And behold, I am with you always, to the end of the age. (Matt. 28:18–20 ESV)

Let me repeat what the Lord says here. "Teaching them to observe all that I have commanded you." It is very important as we read the New Testament, we can see exactly what Jesus commanded them to do. How they worshiped and how often and when did they come together to worship the Lord, how they gave financially, how they observed the Lord's Supper continuously, and so on.

I know there are certain conditions that a Christian may encounter when the burial of a loved one or a friend is not possible. It can even be financial or by the circumstances of their death. I would just simply say this. Burial is my personal choice. I base it upon the Word of God. This subject is not to be taken lightly. I encourage you to do some soul searching as you search the scriptures and then make your decision.

CHAPTER 20

What Is the Unpardonable Sin?

> Therefore I tell you, every sin and blasphemy will be forgiven people, but the blasphemy against the Spirit will not be forgiven. And whoever speaks a word against the Son of Man will be forgiven, but whoever speaks against the Holy Spirit will not be forgiven, either in this age or in the age to come. (Matt. 12:31–32 ESV)

The unpardonable sin or the unforgivable sin has been debated ever since Jesus spoke it. Scholars and theologians have engaged in a spiritual tug of war over it for hundreds and hundreds of years. Some suggest it is cursing God or the Holy Spirit, but no scripture supports that period. Most, however, insist that when one takes their own life or commits suicide that that is the act of unpardonable sin since you can't ask for forgiveness after you have died. So to reach a conclusion based upon truth, we must examine what the scriptures have to say.

The blood of human beings in the Old Testament signifies the sanctity of human life. We are the spiritual property of God. So we know that our lives and the life of it which is the blood is a precious thing to the Lord. The unpardonable sin debate has been going on for hundreds of years. Christ has told us "but whoever speaks against the Holy Spirit will not be forgiven." (Matt. 12:32 ESV)

What truth lies in front of us is the same truth that lies behind us. The holy words of God Almighty. So let us look at some biblical examples.

> A few days later, when Jesus again entered Capernaum, the people heard that he had come home. They gathered in such large numbers that there was no room left, not even outside the door, and he preached the word to them. Some men came, bringing to him a paralyzed man, carried by four of them. Since they could not get him to Jesus because of the crowd, they made an opening in the roof above Jesus by digging through it and then lowered the mat the man was lying on. When Jesus saw their faith, he said to the paralyzed man, "Son, your sins are forgiven." Now some teachers of the law were sitting there, thinking to themselves, "Why does this fellow talk like that? He's blaspheming! Who can forgive sins but God alone?" Immediately Jesus knew in his spirit that this was what they were thinking in their hearts, and he said to them, "Why are you thinking these things? Which is easier: to say to this paralyzed man, 'Your sins are forgiven,' or to say, 'Get up, take your mat and walk'? But I want you to know that the Son of Man has authority on earth to forgive sins." So he said to the man, "I tell you, get up, take your mat and go home." He got up, took his mat and walked out in full view of them all. This amazed everyone and they praised God, saying, "We have never seen anything like this!" (Mark 2:1–12 NIV)

Before going on from this scripture I want to point out an observation. It is not in context with the subject of blasphemy but it is very noteworthy. Mark 2:1 answers a question. Where did Jesus call home? "A few days later, when Jesus again entered Capernaum, the people heard that he had come home." Some people still use Nazareth as his home. The gospel of Matthew tells us that Jesus left Nazareth and went to live in Capernaum after meeting temptation in the wilderness. "Now when he heard that John had been arrested, he withdrew into Galilee. And leaving Nazareth he went and lived in Capernaum by the sea, in the territory of Zebulun and Naphtali" (Matt. 4:12–13 ESV).

Now that the truth has been spoken, we continue to ask ourselves in most cases what is the proper application of what the Lord is saying. We now found ourselves like the twelve who lived with him yet misunderstood him many times when he spoke and he would usually give them a parable or tell them a story to illustrate what he was saying so that they may understand it. We can see in the foregoing scripture in Mark that the Pharisees said it was something that he said when he told the paralyzed man. "Son, your sins are forgiven." We being limited in our knowledge assume by this story in the gospel of Mark that blasphemy must be something you say. Perhaps cursing God or even taking or saying the name of God in vain as it can be done when damning another person with what we consider profanity and it is profanity in a profound way. Those that love the Lord cannot tolerate being around anyone who uses this type of language.

However, the question remains. Is it blasphemy when we use God's name in vain or curse the name of God? The answer is no according to what we have already examined. "And whoever speaks a word against the Son of Man will be forgiven, but whoever speaks against the Holy Spirit will not be forgiven, either in this age or in the age to come" (Matt. 12:31–32 ESV).

We could say that blasphemy must be an action, word, or deed. We already know that it is not a word. Is it an action or deed? We have come to a point where we pray for discernment and that we adhere to what Timothy has written. "Study to shew thyself approved unto

God, a workman that needeth not to be ashamed, rightly dividing the word of truth" (2 Timothy 2:15 KJV).

Jesus told his disciples that when he left this earth that he would send the Holy Spirit.

> Nevertheless, I tell you the truth: it is to your advantage that I go away, for if I do not go away, the Helper will not come to you. But if I go, I will send him to you. And when he comes, he will convict the world concerning sin and righteousness and judgment: concerning sin, because they do not believe in me; concerning righteousness, because I go to the Father, and you will see me no longer. (John 16:7–10 ESV)

This passage tells us that the Holy Spirit was sent by God to spread conviction concerning sin, righteousness, and judgment. Also in John, we read who the Holy Spirit is! "And I will ask the Father, and he will give you another Helper to be with you forever, even the Spirit of truth, whom the world cannot receive because it neither sees him nor knows him. You know him, for he dwells with you and will be in you" (John 14:15–17 ESV). He who receives conviction we already know those convictions come from the Holy Spirit and as Christ has said "even the spirit of truth" attempts to pierce us through and through. As we have learned blaspheming the Holy Spirit is not simply saying something bad about the Holy Spirit. It is the rejection of the conviction of the Holy Spirit who convicts with truth to expose our sin and lead us to the Lord Jesus Christ. When we resist truth, we will veer away from everything holy and be resistful to change or repentance. Without repentance, there is no forgiveness of sin. "I tell you, no! But unless you repent, you too will all perish" (Luke 13:3 NIV). The unforgivable sin of blasphemy against the Spirit is not words spoken in anger. Jesus is only addressing the sin of blasphemy in Matthew and the other gospels. The Lord does not speak of committing suicide or any other sins.

As long as we reject the conviction of the Holy Spirit, we can never find forgiveness for sins. This is why the sin of blasphemy cannot be forgiven. If we never acknowledge our sin and accept the Holy Spirit's offer of salvation, then we will be eternally lost.

Borrowed Body

I do not recall my arrival upon this splendid earth,
Nor my cries of sadness when mother gave me birth.
I came here weak and helpless just a fragile babe,
Born in a borrowed body that lasts me to the grave.
Flesh created by the union of a woman and a man
Mortal and immortality the brainchild of God's plan.
The envy of the angels that behold the father's face
Human in appearance but a soul redeemed by grace.
A borrowed body born that strains on simple words
A heart full of emotion where blood and spirit merge.
A complex combination I'm least but still, I'm most,
A simple human being both flesh and living ghost.
Satan is no stranger to this dust from Adam's seed,
Beloved son named Jesus has died to set me free.
I'm part of all that's living the clay in the potter's hand
The image of my father I'm the reason, I am man.

—Mark Anthony Grubb

About the Author

Mark Anthony Grubb is a published author and poet and Christian speaker. He has appeared and been interviewed on YouTube and Podcasts. His last book had reviews like "Mark Anthony Grubb is a modern David and his words are powerful messages from God. His work has gained attention from people from all walks of life, including people like former president Donald Trump, Johnny Cash, the Carter Family, Florence Henderson, Stephen Hawking, Senator Ted Kennedy, and others."